CW01652773

National Strategy for Neighbourhood Renewal

Report of Policy Action Team 12: Young people

March 2000

© Crown copyright 2000

The text in this document may be reproduced free of charge in any format or media without requiring specific permission. This is subject to the material not being used in a derogatory manner or in a misleading context. The source of the material must be acknowledged as Crown copyright and the title of the document must be included when being reproduced as part of another publication or service.

Contents

Foreword by the Rt Hon Paul Boateng MP, Minister of State at the Home Office and Deputy Home Secretary

I am delighted as Champion Minister for the Policy Action Team on Young People (PAT 12) to be able to introduce this report, which looks at how Government can improve the way policies and services work for young people.

The PAT on Young People was one of 18 teams set up following the Social Exclusion Unit's report on neighbourhood renewal, published in September 1998. The Team included experts from the voluntary sector and business and people with a research background, as well as senior Whitehall officials. I would very much like to thank the Team for the time and effort they have put into this work.

As we enter the 21st century, there can be no more important task facing us than to ensure that, no matter who they are, each young person has the best possible start in life and the opportunity to develop and achieve their full potential. To do so, we must break down the barriers related to gender, ethnic background, disability, or where people live, which too often get in the way.

As the analysis underlying the report graphically illustrates, for a minority of young people, achieving this ambition will not be easy. Through a combination of poverty, family conflict, poor educational opportunities and poor services, too many find themselves apparently destined for a life of underachievement and social exclusion.

Exclusion among young people has emerged as an issue in every Social Exclusion Unit report to date. As a result, a wide range of policy developments is currently in train, most notably the introduction of the Connexions Service, which will guide all young people through the system between the ages of 13 and 19.

Through this and the Sure Start programme, efforts to raise educational standards, the Working Families' Tax Credit and other policies welcomed by the Team in the report, the Government is already making good progress in tackling these problems.

But as the report underlines, there is more to be done.

The Team's recommendations fall into four categories:

- new objectives and structures, to improve the way Government develops and implements policy for young people;
- shifting the balance of effort and resources over time into preventing young people from encountering the worst problems rather than fire-fighting when they are already in deep trouble;
- improving individual services for young people; and
- designing policies around the needs and priorities of young people – not least through involving them in thinking about policies and services and in their delivery.

Many of the recommendations made – on better and more systematic preventive action and on family support and other services for young people, for example – are being considered as part of the cross-cutting review on young people at risk which forms part of the current Spending Review. The results of the Review will be announced in the summer.

The Team has argued that there need to be new mechanisms for Ministers collectively to agree the Government's policies on children and young people, with supporting official arrangements. The Government is currently considering these proposals and will announce exactly how it intends to respond to this aspect of the Team's report following the conclusion of the current Spending Review.

There are no easy answers. However, all of us in the Government believe the proposals made by the Team are the basis for moving forward positively.

Rt Hon PAUL BOATENG MP

Summary

Matthew

Matthew was eight when his father walked out. His relationship with his mother was fine until his step-father moved in a year later. His step-father was very authoritarian and Matthew felt that he seemed to enjoy punishing and humiliating him. As well as being punished by his step-father, Matthew endured frequent beatings from his older half-brother.

Matthew loved some subjects at school, like maths and science, but by secondary school he had problems with reading. He was bullied a lot because he was seen as 'soft', once being beaten unconscious by a group of boys. He was terrified of being in school outside of lessons and to avoid further bullying he began truanting. He also began taking drugs and getting involved in crime.

When he was 16, his mother (at, he believes, his step-father's instigation) kicked him out of his home; for the first night he slept under a railway arch. From then on he went through a series of hostel and B&B accommodation, always having to move on because of some violence, or being threatened, or a place closing down.

Matthew went on a Youth Training Scheme painting and decorating course when he left school. He was living at home at first, but once he left home and began moving from place to place, he dropped out of the course.

When he was 17 he spent six months in jail.

Matthew, now 19, puts much of this down to peer pressure from the group he was hanging around with. He became more heavily involved in drugs, shoplifting and burglary to pay for his drugs that were costing him £45 per day. He described drugs as an "escape from reality".

What is the problem?

1 The purpose of this report is to offer a vision for how the Government can give young people like Matthew a better deal – both supporting them more effectively through adolescence and, if possible, acting earlier to stop them developing problems in the first place.

2 **Chapter 1** sets out how:

- a large minority of young people experience a range of acute problems including illiteracy, homelessness, mental illness, drug addiction and serial offending;
- over the last 20 years, many problems have got worse; and
- on many of these indicators this country is worse than other comparable nations.

3 The box below contains a selection of striking facts:

> One in five children in Britain are growing up in workless households – a higher figure than in any other OECD country;[1]
>
> One in 11 16 to 18 year olds are not in education, training or employment.[2] One in 16 young people leave school without qualifications each year.[3] Alongside Greece and Portugal, the UK has the lowest number of 18 year olds in education in the EU;[4]
>
> Unemployment rates are two to three times higher for young people aged 16–24 from ethnic minority backgrounds, regardless of educational attainment);[5]
>
> Rates of teenage birth are twice that of Germany, three times that of France, and six times that of the Netherlands;[6]
>
> Each year one in five 14–15 year olds spend a night away from home without parental knowledge or permission;[7]
>
> The UK has more 15–16 year old drug users that any other EU country;[8]
>
> One in six 16 to 24 year olds are the victim of a violent offence each year.[9] England and Wales come joint top, with the Netherlands, of 11 industrialised countries for such victimisation.[10]

Why does it happen?

4 The risk of ending up homeless, unemployed or with poor educational qualifications is **not** a lottery. The odds are heavily stacked against those who have experienced multiple disadvantage:

- family life characterised by disrupted relationships, poverty and worklessness;
- education that fails to meet their needs or motivate them;
- peer pressures that encourage sexual activity, drug taking or crime;
- low expectations and the absence of adult role models;
- victimisation and bullying; and
- an inadequate response from public services.

5 Although the exact nature and scale of their exclusion varies among different communities, young black and other ethnic minority people are disproportionately affected by these problems – not least because they are more likely to live in poverty and disadvantaged neighbourhoods. And they also face the additional effects of racism.

6 The impact of these problems falls most heavily on the individuals and families concerned. But it also impacts on all members of society as taxpayers or as victims of crime. **Chapter 6** makes the case, in terms of cost and missed opportunities, for trying to tackle the problem.

How have Government policies contributed to the problem?

7 Some of these problems are the result of broader social and economic changes. But Government policies have not responded as effectively as they could have. There are four key elements:

8 First, the report identifies a number of **critical gaps in individual services**:

- there has not been enough emphasis on prevention, particularly through work with families;
- services have been poorly designed to meet the real circumstances of the poorest young people;
- services have been provided haphazardly or on a restricted basis rather than wherever they are needed and to all who need them; and
- services have failed to adapt to new problems experienced by young people such as poor mental health, drug abuse and family conflict.

9 Second, **money has not always gone to the right place**. In general, Government spending on children increases with increasing deprivation. But there are significant anomalies where children living in some of the most deprived wards have less spent on them than those living in more affluent areas. And for young people (16–24), the state spends on average 14 per cent less money on young people in deprived areas, than on the average young person.[11]

10 Third, policies and services at national and local level have often **failed to consult young people** or involve them in the design and delivery of public services. This contributed to poor policy design and makes young people feel alienated.

11 Fourth, **policymaking and service delivery at national and local level has been fragmented**. Mechanisms to join up public, private and voluntary sector services have been inadequate, with poor co-ordination of the numerous players.

12 This has meant that services and departments have too often worked in isolation or at cross purposes, evaded responsibility for the individual, and failed to harness each other's skills. Young people have been dumped from agency to agency, only to be picked up once they hit a crisis.

What can be done?

13 Despite the magnitude of the problem, the Policy Action Team (PAT) believes that an effective approach to the problems experienced by young people **can** be developed.

14 First, a lot is known about the factors that mean young people are at great risk.

15 Second, a lot is known about what works in reducing these factors and helping young people overcome the odds. Research[12] shows that where young people have clear and high expectations, trusting relationships with adult role models, participation in out-of-school activities and in family life, a mentor, and where they receive recognition and praise, they thrive.

16 The PAT believes that this knowledge is not applied often enough. Young people with multiple risk factors are often not picked up early enough. It is rarely anyone's job to do this. And effective approaches are neither evaluated nor disseminated. The Team's proposals are designed to overcome these failures.

The PAT's proposals

17 The PAT recognises that many changes introduced by this Government are already making a real difference on the ground, and that others will make a difference in the future. The PAT particularly welcomes:

- the Government's commitment to end child poverty in 20 years, and halve it in ten;
- Sure Start for young children;
- the school standards agenda, tackling the problem of failing schools;
- the strengthening of Children's Services Plans;
- action to modernise services for vulnerable children, including those in care, through Quality Protects;
- better-designed services for specific groups of young people, for example through Youth Offending Teams and Drug Action Teams;
- the commitment to establish a new universal youth support service, Connexions; and
- the New Deal for Young People.

18 The PAT therefore believes that the key challenge is to achieve greater coherence at a national and local level of existing initiatives, rather than invent a series of new ones.

19 The recommendations set out below are currently being considered in the Spending Review on Youth at Risk.

A youth policy

20 A key conclusion of this report is the need for greater coherence of Government policies at a national and local level. The PAT recommends that **Youth Inclusion Objectives should be established at national level** and reflected in departmental policies.

21 These objectives should be championed by a **Ministerial Group for Young People** which would have an overview of youth policy, and be responsible for implementing youth policy objectives.

22 This should have dedicated official support, perhaps in the form of a '**Youth Unit**' whose responsibilities would include: driving forward implementation of cross-Government objectives; assembling knowledge on young people and 'what works'; supporting Ministers in refining the youth strategy, including simplifying the number of initiatives and plans; and drawing together an annual report on the Government's strategy for youth inclusion, with the Government making time for this to be debated in Parliament.

23 The PAT believes a more effective and coherent approach nationally needs to be matched locally. The key roles for local co-ordination include: identifying the local needs of young people; promoting a common assessment framework for young people; sharing information between agencies; identifying public, private and voluntary resources which could help young people; and developing a local youth strategy, based on effective consultation.

Prevention

24 To help shift resources into prevention, the PAT argues for improved **support for families**. This would mean a new approach to helping parents and children deal with problems before they become acute, increasing the availability and take-up of a range of family services, from school-family partnerships and parental self-help groups, to family mediation, therapy and counselling.

25 The PAT also advocates a new **preventive budget** to promote effective cross-cutting interventions for young people facing the most acute risks. The rewards of effective prevention often do not fall on the organisation or department that was responsible for producing it. A ring-fenced preventive budget would ensure that important preventive activities are properly funded.

Making individual services better

26 The PAT found evidence that some critical services were absent or under great pressure in areas where they were badly needed. Examples include: mental and sexual health, alcohol and drugs misuse, leisure, the education of offenders, benefits, housing and volunteering. For instance, the Audit Commission has found that spending on mental health services varies by a factor of seven. The Spending Review needs to make a start on correcting this.

A new approach to designing and delivering services

27 The PAT suggests that young people need to be much more closely involved in the way services are designed and delivered. It sets out thinking on how the involvement of young people can be made an integral part of the new approach to youth inclusion, and on how this can be done effectively. It recommends that:

- all Government departments, agencies and local government should have a policy of consulting and involving young people in policy development and service delivery; and

- the 'Youth Unit' or other cross-cutting mechanism should facilitate this and set out in its annual reports what has been done.

Conclusion

28 The PAT's work has highlighted a range of deep-seated problems affecting too many young people. The task for turning this round may seem huge, but the PAT believes that policies already in place or in the pipeline represent an important start. And there are huge resources to be tapped in public, voluntary and private sectors, never mind communities, parents and young people themselves. The task now is to pull all this together so that whole is more than the sum of its parts. That is the key message of this report.

Part I – Young people at risk today

Chapter 1: The problem – nature, scale and causes

A significant minority of young people today experience a wide range of problems and acute crises in adolescence. The scale of these problems is in many cases worse than this country's past experience and worse than other apparently comparable countries. The problems are concentrated in, but not confined to, the most deprived neighbourhoods. There is an increasing body of knowledge about the risk factors that increase the likelihood of experiencing acute crises, and the protective factors that help young people overcome the odds.

Focus of this report

1.1 The findings in the Social Exclusion Unit's (SEU's) 1998 report on neighbourhood renewal[13] are the starting point for this report:

- the poorest neighbourhoods contain disproportionate numbers of young people;
- poor education and poor opportunities are common problems for young people in poor neighbourhoods; and
- young people are often perceived as a problem by other residents and agencies.

1.2 This PAT was set up to look at why these things happen and what can be done about them.

1.3 Research shows that just as many young people who experience poverty, poor family support, low educational attainment and other problems live outside deprived neighbourhoods as in them.[14] The PAT therefore decided that its report needed to look at disadvantage among young people wherever they live. Deprived neighbourhoods remain, however, an important part of the picture.

1.4 The PAT generally saw the 13–19 year old group as the focus for its study of young people. But it also decided that it would not make sense to adopt a rigorous age threshold for its work, since so many problems have their roots in earlier years and continue to impact on young people's lives into their twenties and beyond.

1.5 All of the 18 PATs were asked to look specifically at race as an aspect of exclusion. (The full remit of PAT 12 is at **Annex A.**) This issue is as critical for young people as it is for the issues addressed by other PATs. The analysis and recommendations in this report reflect the way that race is central to the experience of exclusion for many young people. **Annex C** brings together what the PAT has found on race.

Context

Changes in the economy and society

1.6 Young people today face a markedly different situation to their predecessors, and one that is still rapidly changing. Many of the changes experienced by most young people have been positive: most are better educated, more wealthy, physically healthier and live longer.[15] However, there are also changes – particularly in the nature of the labour market, family relationships and social structures – that mean young people face new risks and challenges:

- **far more jobs now only open to those with qualifications.**[16] Most young people therefore spend more time in learning, but there are fewer opportunities for those without skills;
- **the disappearance of traditional sources of employment**[17] and less likelihood of a 'job for life'.[18] While some welcome the prospect of periodic job change and acquiring new skills to learn throughout a working life, for others it is a threat;
- **longer dependence on parental support**[19] as young people enter work, marry and leave the parental home later in life;
- **earlier and more intense exposure to high risk behaviour,**[20] including experimentation with alcohol, smoking, drugs and sex, and exposure to violence;
- **social and media attitudes** encouraging pre-adolescents and adolescents to be seen as older than they are and behave accordingly;
- **greater likelihood of experiencing breakdown in their own relationships** with one in four marriages likely to end in divorce;[21] and
- **racism, with a more diverse population of young people**, concentrated in the poorest places. Those from ethnic minority groups very often experience greater poverty, poorer public services and in some cases specific challenges like the need to learn English or recover from the trauma of being a refugee.[22]

Weaker support mechanisms

1.7 At the same time the support mechanisms on which adolescents have traditionally depended have been weakened in some significant and overlapping ways:

- for many young people, **family ties** have become more fluid or more fragile. One in four children born in the 1970s experienced the break-up of their parents' marriage by the age of 16.[23] One in 12 children currently live in step-parent families and around one in five children live in single parent families, three times the number in 1971.[24] And over the last ten years, contact with grandparents and other relatives also fell.[25] (The trends relating to families are explored in more depth in **Annex D**);
- **community ties** too may be of less help to young people, particularly where a whole neighbourhood has suffered entrenched long-term unemployment and so role models and informal networks are either limited or provide a negative influence;
- there is **less access, in schools and elsewhere, to help with problems in learning or personal life because of limitations on resources and the priority given to the most acute problems**; and

- by far the most powerful factor has been the effect of **growing inequality in income and employment**. In 1995–96, one in three children grew up in poverty, compared with one in ten in 1979.[26] One in five households have no family member in work.[27]

The effect on young people: more young people unable to cope

1.8 The result of all these changes has been dramatic:

- a significant minority of young people experience a range of serious problems and acute crises in adolescence;
- the numbers affected are in many cases worse than other comparable countries; and
- too many of the trends have been in the wrong direction.

1.9 The boxes below set out the headlines.

Scale

- One in 16 young people leave school without qualifications each year.[28]
- One in five school children have Special Educational Needs (SEN), but less than one in six of these children have statements that set out what these needs are and how they should be met.[29]
- One in 11 16–18 year olds are not in education, employment or training at any one time.[30]
- One in five 14–15 year olds spend a night away from home without parental knowledge or permission each year.[31]
- One in five 16–24 year olds experience homelessness at some time in their lives.[32]
- One in four 18–25 year olds and one in 12 16–17 year olds drink alcohol three or more times a week.[33]
- One in nine 11–15 year olds and one in three 16–19 year olds smoke regularly.[34]
- One in two 16–19 year olds have tried drugs.[35]
- One in 14 16–24 year olds have tried cocaine.[36]
- One in six 16–24 year olds will be the victim of a violent offence in any one year.[37]
- One in two prisoners under 18 have been looked after children.[38]

½ prisoners under 18 were in care.

European comparisons

- Alongside Greece and Portugal, the UK has the lowest number of 18 year olds in learning in the EU.[39]
- With the exception of Portugal, the UK has the highest proportion of school leavers in the EU with no more than Level 2 qualifications. This proportion is nearly 50 per cent above the EU average.[40]
- One in five children in Britain are growing up in workless households – a higher figure than in any other OECD country.[41]
- Rates of teenage birth are twice that of Germany, three times that of France, six times that of the Netherlands.[42]
- The UK has more 15–16 year old drug users than any other EU country.[43]
- England and Wales come joint top, with the Netherlands, of 11 industrialised countries for victimisation.[44]

Trends

- At the end of the 1970s, one in ten children lived in poor households. Today it is one in three.[45]
- At the end of the 1970s, around seven per cent of children lived in households with no adult in work; by 1995–96 this number had risen to 21 per cent.[46]
- The proportion of pupils with an SEN statement has increased by 60 per cent since the late 1980s.[47]
- Permanent exclusions from school have risen from 4,000 per year in 1991–92 to over 12,000 in 1997–98.[48]
- Between the mid-1980s and mid-1990s, referrals for self-harm by young people increased by a third.
- The prevalence of drug use among 12–13 year olds has increased fivefold and among 14–15 year olds eightfold since 1987.[49]
- Overall involvement of young people as victims of crime increased by 75 per cent between the early 1980s and the mid-1990s.[50]
- Young men are growing out of property crime later: the peak age of offending has risen from 15 in 1986 to 18 in 1994.[51]

1.10 **Table 1** sets out all these facts in more detail by subject.

Table 1: Young people's problems – scale, trends and international comparisons

NB: The notes for this table can be found at **Annex E**.

Issue	*Scale [1,2]*	*Trends [3]*	*Gender, ethnic minority, at-risk groups and area concentrations [4]*	*International comparisons [5]*
Education, employment and training				
Underachievement at school	One in 16 young people (nearly 40,000) leave school without qualifications each year, of whom more than 80 per cent are not entered for exams. [6]	Although the proportion of 16–17 year olds with no qualifications has declined since the late 1980s, it is now levelling out and the gap between those who achieve in school and those who do not is widening. [7]	Boys (especially at primary level). Ethnic minorities (except Indian and Chinese). [8] Persistent truants, those excluded from school and looked after children. [9,10] One in four children in secondary schools serving difficult-to-let estates gain no qualifications. [11] Schools with high proportions of children with free school meals. [12]	With the exception of Portugal, the UK has the highest proportion of school leavers in the EU with no more than Level 2 qualifications, which is nearly 50 per cent above the EU average. [13]
Special Educational Needs (SEN)	One in five children have SEN. [14]	The proportion of pupils with an SEN statement has increased by 60 per cent since the late 1980s. For those with no statement, the numbers have increased by 30 per cent since 1996. [15]	Schools with high proportions of children eligible for free school meals. [16] Deprived areas. [17]	Higher rates than in Canada, Denmark, Germany, Iceland, Italy and the US. [18]
Illiteracy/innumeracy	In Britain, 17 per cent of 16–25 year olds have literacy problems and 22 per cent have numeracy problems. [19]	No recent trend data, but levels of literacy and numeracy among 15–16 year olds changed little between the late 1970s and the late 1980s. [20,21]	Boys: literacy (just worse); girls: numeracy (much worse). [22] Those with English as a second language. Deprived areas. [23] Areas with high proportions of poor ethnic minority residents. [24]	In a comparison of literacy and numeracy levels in 12 similarly industrialised countries, only two countries – Poland and Ireland – had lower levels than in Britain. [25]

Table 1: Young people's problems – scale, trends and international comparisons

Issue	*Scale* [1,2]	*Trends* [3]	*Gender, ethnic minority, at-risk groups and area concentrations* [4]	*International comparisons* [5]
Education, employment and training (continued)				
Truancy	In England and Wales, more than 30,000 children in Year 11 truant for days or weeks at a time [26] and in England about 60,000 truant at least once a week. [27]	No significant change in the last ten years in rates of persistent truancy in England and Wales (days or weeks at a time). [28]	Young homeless and traveller children. [29] Young offenders. [30] Local authority housing and inner city areas. Schools with similar intakes have very different truancy rates. [31] Schools serving difficult-to-let estates. [32]	No comparative data.
School exclusions	There are 1,500 permanent exclusions from primary schools and 11,500 permanent exclusions from secondary schools per year. [33] More than 150,000 young people are out of school on fixed term exclusion (1–45 days) at any one time. [34]	400 per cent increase in permanent exclusion from primary schools since 1990–91, but stable since 1995. 350 per cent increase in secondary school permanent exclusions since 1990–91, but small drop since 1997–98. [35] No trend data on fixed term exclusions.	Boys. Black Caribbean, Black African and mixed race. Looked after children and children with SEN and Emotional and Behavioural Difficulties and the young homeless. [36] Young offenders. [37] Schools in difficulty, predominantly in deprived areas and inner and outer London. [38]	No comparative data.

Table 1: Young people's problems – scale, trends and international comparisons

Issue	*Scale* [1,2]	*Trends* [3]	*Gender, ethnic minority, at-risk groups and area concentrations* [4]	*International comparisons* [5]
Education, employment and training (continued)				
Not participating post-16	170,000 16–18 year olds (over nine per cent) are not in education, employment or training at any one time. [39]	Rose with recession in the 1990s and has not fallen back. [40] Twenty years ago, nearly half of school leavers went into jobs, whereas today it is less than ten per cent. [41]	Boys. Pakistani, Bangladeshi and African Caribbean young people. Deprived neighbourhoods. [42]	Alongside Greece and Portugal, the UK has the lowest number of 18 year olds in education in the EU. [43]
Unemployment post-18	In Britain, more than eight per cent (nearly 300,000) of 18–24 year olds are unemployed, of whom 20 per cent have been unemployed for six months or more. [44]	After rising to over 700,000 at the beginning of the 1990s, the unemployment rate among 18–24 year olds has nearly halved. The number unemployed for six months or more has fallen steeply since the early 1990s. [45]	Boys (girls more likely to be economically inactive). Ethnic minorities. [46] Deprived areas (especially coalfields, some rural areas and areas of high structural unemployment).	The rate of youth unemployment (16–24 year olds) is above the EU average, but lower than in Finland, France, Greece, Italy and Spain. [47]

Table 1: Young people's problems – scale, trends and international comparisons

Issue	*Scale* [1,2]	*Trends* [3]	*Gender, ethnic minority, at-risk groups and area concentrations* [4]	*International comparisons* [5]
Housing and the transition to independent living				
Homelessness and running away from home	There are approximately 32,000 homeless 16–21 year olds in Britain. [48] A fifth of 16–24 year olds experience homelessness at some time in their lives. [49] More than 100,000 16–17 year olds claim severe hardship payments annually. [50] 77,000 (one in nine) 14–15 year olds run away from home each year, of whom about 11,000 stay away for a week or more.[51]	Youth homelessness has increased substantially since the 1970s. [52] Claims for severe hardship payments rose from 1988 to 1996 and have declined since then. [53] The number of young people leaving home due to family problems is also increasing. [54] No trend data on runaways.	Homeless (18–24 year old) – boys; runaways (14–15 year old) – girls. Nearly half of all the young homeless people in London are from Black African, Black Caribbean and other ethnic minority groups. [55] Verbally or physically abusive parent(s). [56] Care leavers. [57] Children from step-families, those with SEN and those looked after are over-represented amongst runaways. [58]	16–17 year olds are disproportionately homeless in the UK compared with other EU countries. [59]
Young carers	There are 20,000 to 50,000 carers in the UK aged under 18,[60] half of whom are aged 11–15. [61]	No trend data.	Girls, who are especially more likely to undertake domestic tasks and intimate care. [62] Young carers from ethnic minorities, particularly girls, are more likely to care for someone who is not a parent or sibling and more likely to provide intimate care. [63] Children in lone parent families. [64] Those bullied at school. [65]	No comparative data. [66]

Table 1: Young people's problems – scale, trends and international comparisons

Issue	*Scale* [1,2]	*Trends* [3]	*Gender, ethnic minority, at-risk groups and area concentrations* [4]	*International comparisons* [5]
Housing and the transition to independent living (continued)				
Young people looked after	There are 370,000 children at any one time defined as 'in need' under the Children Act, 1989. [67] There are 55,300 children (five per 1,000) currently looked after by their local authority, of whom 6,300 are in children's homes. [68]	The long-term decline in the number of looked after children stopped in 1994 and has since that time risen by 11 per cent. [69]	Boys (slightly). [70] Those of mixed race. [71] Children from ethnic minorities make up one-fifth of looked after children. [72]	No comparative data.
Health				
Teenage conceptions	There are 90,000 teenage conceptions a year, 7,700 to under-16s. [73]	Under-20 conceptions generally stick at level of mid-1970s or higher. [74] The proportion of teenage conceptions outside of marriage has risen from 40 per cent in 1978 to 90 per cent currently. [75]	Pakistani, Bangladeshi and African Caribbean young people. Looked after children, persistent truants and school excludees. [76, 77] Deprived neighbourhoods. [78]	Overall, figures have not fallen in line with other European countries. Teenage birth rates are twice that of Germany, three times that of France, six times that of the Netherlands. [79]
Mental health, including suicide	In England and Wales about 600 (10 per 100,000) 15–24 year olds take their own life each year, i.e. more than 10,000 since 1982. [80] Up to 20,000 teenagers go to hospital each year as a consequence of deliberate self-harm. [81]	Young people account for a considerably higher proportion of all suicides than 20 years ago. During the 1980s, suicides among 15–24 year old males increased by 75 per cent, but during the 1990s have fallen slightly. [82] From the mid-1980s to the mid-1990s, the number of under-19s referred for self-harm rose by about a third. Depression increasing with younger age of onset. [83]	Boys: suicide. [84] Girls: self-harm, depression and eating disorders. Unemployed. [85] Looked after children. Persistent young offenders. Deprived and inner city areas. [86] Homeless young people almost three times more likely to experience mental health problems, which are more likely to be chronic and severe. A third of young homeless people have attempted suicide. [87]	Although higher than some countries (Greece, Italy, Spain, the Netherlands and Portugal), the suicide rate amongst young people aged 15–24 in the UK is lower than in most other EU countries. [88] Levels of loneliness, depression and school stress are higher in England and Wales than some EU countries (e.g. Denmark, Germany and Austria), but lower than in others (e.g. Northern Ireland, Finland and France). [89]

Table 1: Young people's problems – scale, trends and international comparisons

Issue	*Scale* [1,2]	*Trends* [3]	*Gender, ethnic minority, at-risk groups and area concentrations* [4]	*International comparisons* [5]
Health (continued)				
Disability	In the UK, around 360,000 (three per cent) of children aged 0–16 have a disability. Nearly two-thirds have more than one disability. [90] Around 10 per cent of 16–19 year olds have a current long-term disability (GB figure). The main types are chest and breathing problems (35 per cent). [91]	No trend data.	Boys. [92] Children over 5. [93]	No comparative data.
Drug use	In England and Wales, half (i.e. more than one million) of all 16–19 year olds have tried drugs. [94] Over 100,000 have tried opiates plus [95] and some 700,000 have tried hallucinogens [96]. About 400,000 16–24 year olds (seven per cent) have tried cocaine. [97] The number of acute drug-related deaths increased by 50 per cent from 1988 to 1995. [98] Among young men, deaths from drug abuse doubled between 1993 and 1997. [99]	The prevalence of drug use among 12–13 year olds has increased fivefold and among 14–15 year olds eightfold since 1987, but now appears to be levelling off. [100,101] In recent years, drug use among young people aged 16–29 has begun to level off, but cocaine use is increasing sharply. [102] The age of onset for drug use is getting younger. [103] Poly-drug use and mixing drug and alcohol use is becoming more common. [104]	Older boys (particularly cocaine – nearly twice as many). [105] Truants, the young homeless, children excluded from school, looked after children and children with emotional and behavioural difficulties. [106] London (cocaine). Deprived areas (especially problem drug use (particularly heroin) and drug-related problems). [107,108] Council and inner city housing. [109]	The UK has more 15–16 year old drug users than any other EU country. [110]

Table 1: Young people's problems – scale, trends and international comparisons

Issue	*Scale* [1,2]	*Trends* [3]	*Gender, ethnic minority, at-risk groups and area concentrations* [4]	*International comparisons* [5]
Health (continued)				
Alcohol use	60 per cent of 15 year olds have been drunk at least twice. One in four 18–25 year olds and one in 12 16–17 year olds drink alcohol three or more times a week. [111] About ten per cent of young men aged 18–24 are alcohol dependent. [112]	Steep rise in under-age drinking since 1990, especially among boys, but now signs of levelling off. Amount drunk by 11–15 year old drinkers doubled from 1990 to 1998. [113] The proportion of young women aged 18–24 who drink regularly (i.e. more than 14 units per week) increased from 15 per cent to 22 per cent from 1984 to 1996. [114]	Under 18, boys are slightly more likely to drink regularly and consume more than girls; among 18–24 year olds, twice as many men are heavy drinkers as women. [115] White young people more likely to drink than young people from ethnic minorities. [116]	The proportion of 15 year olds who have been drunk at least twice (at least 60 per cent) is higher in England and Wales than elsewhere in Europe, except Denmark.
Smoking	About 11 per cent (339,000) 11–15 year olds [117] and about one in three (over 700,000) 16–19 year olds smoke regularly. [118]	Steep rise in number of 11–15 year old regular smokers since late 1980s, but two per cent decline since 1996 to 11 per cent. [119]	Females. [120]	In a study of 28 countries, England are in the top third for regular (daily) smoking by children aged 11, 13 and 15. [121]

Table 1: Young people's problems – scale, trends and international comparisons

Issue	*Scale* [1,2]	*Trends* [3]	*Gender, ethnic minority, at-risk groups and area concentrations* [4]	*International comparisons* [5]
Victimisation and offending				
Victim of crime	In England and Wales, young people aged 16–24 are more likely to be victimised than any other group. For example, a quarter of all violent crime is committed against young men. [122] 28 per cent of young women aged 20–24 admit being assaulted by a partner at some time, 34 per cent threatened or assaulted. Figures for 16–19 year olds are 15 and 20 per cent respectively. [123] One in six young people aged 14–25 are the victim of a violent offence each year [124] and more than one in three 12–15 year olds are assaulted each year. [125] Over 15,000 children contact ChildLine each year to talk about sexual or physical abuse. One or two children die each week as a result of abuse or neglect. [126]	A 75 per cent rise in overall victimisation between the early 1980s and the mid-1990s, after which there has been a small decline. [127]	Boys and young men. Disabled and those with learning difficulties disproportionately at risk of abuse. [128] Areas of physical disrepair. Households headed by young people, especially in inner cities. [129]	England and Wales (together with the Netherlands) have higher rates of victimisation than in 11 other industrialised countries. It also has the highest rate of fear of crime. [130]

Table 1: Young people's problems – scale, trends and international comparisons

Issue	*Scale* [1,2]	*Trends* [3]	*Gender, ethnic minority, at-risk groups and area concentrations* [4]	*International comparisons* [5]
Victimisation and offending (continued)				
Offending	One in three men have a criminal record by the age of 30. [131] 40 per cent of offenders are under the age of 21 and a quarter are under 18. [132]	Increase in violent crime by juveniles (especially young women) and young adults. Peak age of offending has risen from 15 in 1986 to 18 in 1994. [133] Young men growing out of property crime later. [134]	African-Caribbean young men over-represented at every stage of the criminal justice process, from stop and search to imprisonment. [135] Deprived areas. [136]	Sharper rise in violence by juvenile girls than in ten other European countries. [137]
Young people in custody	There are 11,500 15–21 year olds in custody,[138] of whom at least three-quarters will be re-convicted within two years of release. [139] Nearly three-quarters of offenders under the age of 21 released from prison are re-convicted within two years. [140]	The imprisonment rate has risen by about 50 per cent since the early 1990s. [141]	On reception: • 25 per cent of young male prisoners are homeless or have been living in insecure accommodation; • over half under 18 had been looked after or had contact with social services; • over half 15–17 year olds had been excluded from school; • nearly two-thirds have no qualifications (80 per cent of 15–17 year olds), and two-thirds are unemployed on entry to custody; • almost two-thirds misuse drugs and a quarter claimed current or past drinking problem (three-quarters of whom had never received any help); • one in six admitted to having been abused and one in ten admitted to self-harm; • nearly a quarter are fathers or expectant fathers. [142]	Of 29 member states of the Council of Europe, only Romania, Estonia and Lithuania have higher rates of imprisonment than England for young people under the age of 21. [143]

General risk factors

1.11 It is not a lottery who will experience these problems. **Table 2** sets out the key risk factors drawing on research conducted all over the world into the nature and causes of young people's problems:

Table 2: Key risk factors for adolescent problems[52]

Risk factors	Adverse outcomes					
	Drug abuse	*Youth crime*	*School-age pregnancy*	*School failure*	*Mental health problems*	*Homelessness*
Family						
Poor parenting	●	●	●	●	●	●
Family conflict	●	●	●	●	●	●
Low income and poor housing	●	●	●	●	●	●
In care	●	●	●	●	●	●
School						
Low achievement	●	●	●	●	●	●
Truancy	●	●	●	●		●
Exclusion	●	●	●	●	●	●
Community						
Disadvantaged neighbourhood	●	●	●	●	●	●
Friends condoning or involved in risky behaviour	●	●	●	●		

1.12 The experience of one or more risk factors does not *automatically* lead to poor outcomes. Risk factor analysis is not an exact science and poor outcomes are more likely with exposure to some risks than to others. But the probabilities can get very high for young people who have several risk factors as **Figures 1** and **2** show:

Figure 1: Probability of delinquency[53]

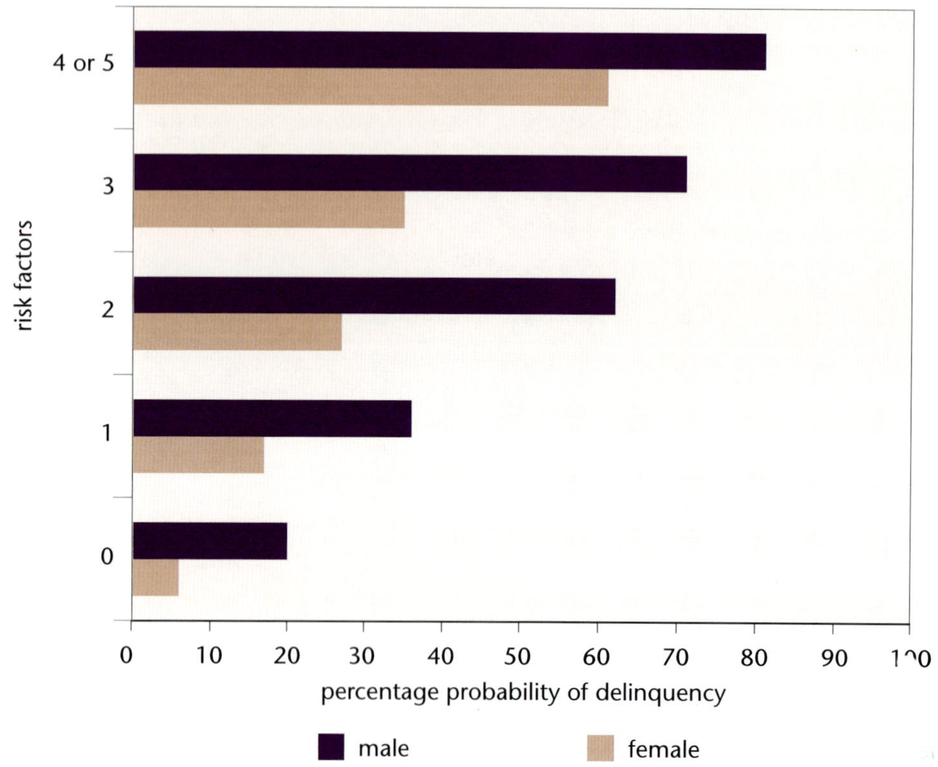

Figure 2: Probability of teenage motherhood[54]

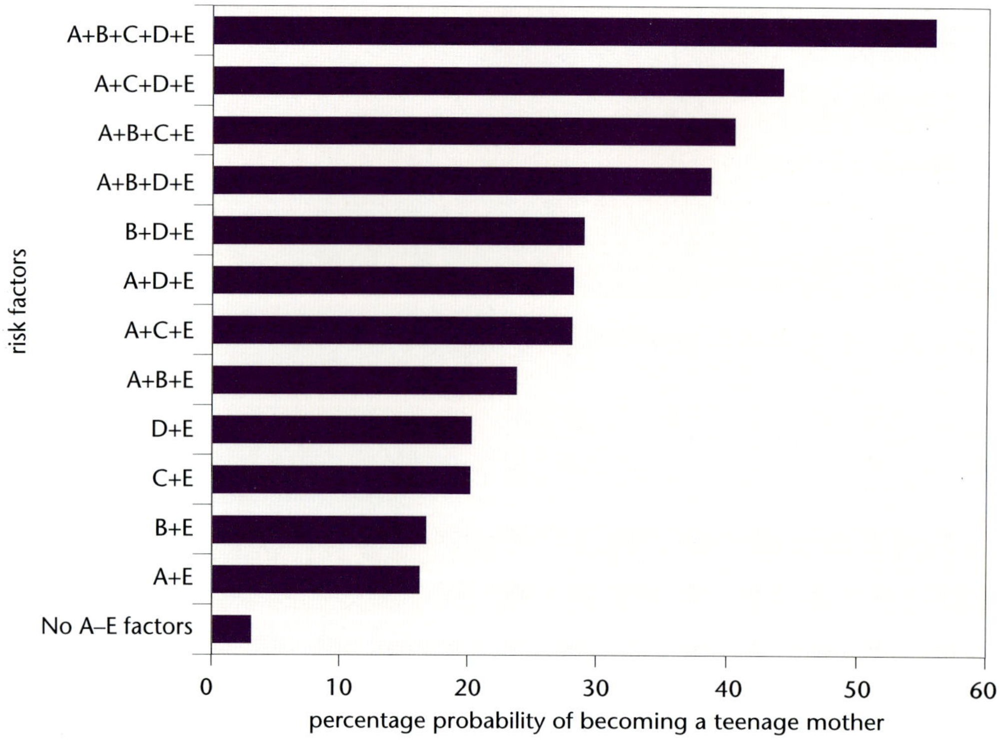

A: emotional problems aged 7 or 16; B: mother was a teenage mother; C: families who experienced financial adversity when the teenage mother was aged 7 or 16; D: preference for being a young mother; E: low educational attainment aged 16.

Is there an area phenomenon?

1.13 Almost all the problems listed in **Table 1** tend to hit young people in deprived neighbourhoods hardest. The PAT believes there are a number of reasons for this, including: the clustering of people on low incomes; higher levels of unemployment; and higher levels of failing schools. Each young person in a deprived area is more likely to experience the effects of these in their own lives and through the influence of their peer group.

Are boys more at risk than girls?

1.14 As **Table 1** shows, boys seem more likely than girls to experience many of the visible problems associated with social exclusion – educational underachievement, exclusion from school, unemployment, crime and homelessness. However, girls may be at equal risk, all the more because the problems which they fall victim to (such as eating disorders) may not attract attention.

1.15 For some issues, such as SEN, truancy and under-age drinking, the differences are marginal or non-existent, while for other issues, such as teenage parenthood, smoking, sexual abuse and some kinds of mental ill-health (depression, self-harm, eating disorders), the evidence shows that girls are more at risk than boys. In poor neighbourhoods, the differences are less stark. Educationally, for example, girls in such neighbourhoods do not outperform boys to the same extent as nationally.

Is there an ethnic minority effect?

1.16 **Table 1** also demonstrates that young people from some ethnic minority backgrounds are disproportionately at risk of experiencing many of these problems. The box below shows some of the facts.

Young people from ethnic minority backgrounds

- Children from ethnic minorities make up one-fifth of looked after children,[55] but only around one-tenth of the under-18 population as a whole.
- Although no more likely to be persistent truants, African-Caribbean pupils are five times more likely to be excluded from school and up to 15 times more likely in some inner city areas.[56]
- Regardless of level of qualification, nationally rates of unemployment are two to three times higher for young people aged 16–24 from ethnic minority backgrounds (and in some areas very much higher).[57]
- Four per cent of Modern Apprentices are black, compared with a population benchmark of eight per cent.[58]
- It generally takes more job referrals to move a young ethnic minority person on the New Deal into work, compared to a white young person.[59]
- Nearly half of those using Centrepoint's temporary housing services are black.[60]
- Black people are significantly over-represented in 'stop and searches', among arrests and among those sent to prison.[61]

1.17 The PAT concluded that there are two effects at work here:

- racism and discrimination in their own right; and
- the fact that young people from some ethnic minority backgrounds are more likely to experience other risk factors such as poverty, being looked after or living in deprived neighbourhoods.

Protective factors

1.18 Many young people manage to overcome the risks and obstacles they face. Evaluations of programmes for young people[62] have identified a consistent set of factors that help young people overcome disadvantage. These include:

- strong relationships with parents, family members, teachers and other significant adults;
- clear, high expectations;
- mentoring and positive role models;
- individual characteristics: outgoing nature, self-motivation, resilience and intelligence;
- active involvement in families, school life and community life, for example, participation in out-of-school learning programmes;
- recognition and praise; and
- parental interest and involvement in education.

1.19 Research shows that where problems have occurred, things can be turned around. For example, young people who have offended can desist from doing so again for a variety of reasons, such as moving away from those who have been a negative influence, entering into a stable relationship, or being given a new sense of direction and purpose by going into education, employment or training.[63]

1.20 Nevertheless, the analysis above clearly makes the case for Government policies that are aimed at strengthening the protective factors and reducing the risk factors.

1.21 Many policies have this as their aim already. However, **Chapter 5** shows how a number of other Government policies lack a strong enough focus on prevention.

Chapter 2: How does it feel?

This chapter uses real life case studies to show how the problems discussed in Chapter 1 impact on the everyday lives of young people and their families.

2.1 The cases given below are those of real young people: only their names have been changed. They are not a typology of disengaged young people. Each young person's circumstances are different. But they show the range and intensity of obstacles that many young people face and offer a glimpse of what disadvantage means in some real cases. And they show that even seemingly insurmountable problems are often overcome.

2.2 As explained elsewhere in this report, many of the problems experienced by young people in their late teens or early twenties (and beyond) can be traced back to events that happened to them in early childhood. Sometimes these are sudden and traumatic, like bereavement or divorce of their parents, sometimes simply the result of the environment in which the young person grows up. The cases of Lisa, Michael, and Wayne[64] show this well.

Lisa

Lisa is now 18. Her father died when she was seven. She had a difficult relationship with her mother, which worsened when her mother's boyfriend moved in when Lisa was 11. Lisa felt that he led her mother to be stricter with her than would have otherwise been the case.

Lisa ran away from home when she was 11, only returning when she got hungry. She started smoking and by the age of 14 had been arrested for being drunk. She also started shoplifting and was arrested twice, though not charged. Her relationship at home deteriorated and her mother threw her out when she was 15.

She spent a month in a children's home and then went on to foster parents from whom she ran away. She was eventually returned, but then moved on to a different couple whom she 'hated'. She ran away again after four months. She stopped going to school and wasn't entered for any exams. Having lived with friends for six months – among other things looking after their children – Lisa moved into a hostel, where she began taking drugs. Nine months later she moved into a housing association flat, but then she became pregnant. The flat was too small, so she was offered and accepted a council flat.

Suffering from depression, she dropped out of a training course in hairdressing, and took up a poorly paid job waitressing in a café while still signing on for benefits.

Michael

Several members of Michael's family have a criminal record. He is currently long-term excluded from his third school. He does not keep his appointments with the Educational Welfare Service. He is given £1 dinner money a day and told to keep out of the house. He lives with his step-father, who is unemployed. His step-father says that he can't control Michael's aggressive and anti-social behaviour. Michael's biological father, on the other hand, does not challenge it. Michael drinks and smokes cannabis from time to time. Michael is ten.

Wayne

Wayne lived with his mother, father and two brothers until he was five, when his parents split up. His father left, taking his two brothers with him. Wayne's mother remarried, but he never got on with his step-father, who was very strict and soon began to physically abuse him. Wayne felt he had no-one to talk to about this.

Things got worse after a new baby arrived when Wayne was eight, and after one particular beating, he ran away from home for the first time. Although he returned, there soon developed a pattern of running away to escape the arguments and physical abuse. With their attention on the new child, Wayne felt that his family didn't care that he had run away. Often he would sleep in the park or down by the canal. At the age of 11, he ran away from home again, this time in an attempt to track down his natural father. Altogether he ran away 14 times between the ages of eight and 11.

Eventually it was decided that it might be better for him to move in with his natural father. By this time, Wayne had fallen behind with his education, and at his new school he felt isolated and began to truant regularly. He started to misuse drugs and alcohol and was finally excluded for starting a fire in a classroom.

Things rapidly went downhill. Wayne got involved in car theft and his father threw him out. Aged 15, he was then put into foster care and things improved. He felt that his foster parents were more understanding and that he was able to talk to them.

Given the success of his foster placement, it was felt that Wayne would be able to progress to independent accommodation. Wayne was immediately inundated by friends asking to sleep over. Drug-taking became common and he soon relapsed into drug abuse, falling quickly into debt and rent arrears. Wayne felt he had no option but to leave the area.

2.3 Where a young person is exhibiting signs of going 'off-track', there is no single response; a dizzying range of different agencies and individuals might step in. Each has a valuable contribution to make, but too often none will see the whole picture.

2.4 Take for example the case of Michael, above. He is well on course over the next couple of years to come into contact with school teachers, special needs/pupil referral teachers, an educational welfare officer, the Careers Service, the police, the local Youth Offending Team (YOT), drugs prevention projects (statutory/voluntary), social worker, youth worker (statutory/voluntary), nurses, casualty staff and the local GP.

2.5 In Michael's case, the influence of his family, and an environment of criminal activity, is obviously not beneficial. But some young people may fail to reach their full potential through less obvious family pressures.

> ### *Jason*
>
> At 16, Jason has no qualifications and only a limited network of friends and family. He lives at home with his unemployed mother and three brothers and sisters. He does not want to return to education, and stacks shelves at the local supermarket for £1 an hour. This is his full-time occupation; and on £37 per week he is still better off than on benefit because he lives at home.
>
> But Jason is regarded positively by his friends and family because he has obtained work that sets him above his peers; he has some real income. He cannot see the greater rewards that might arise if he were to gain some qualifications. His mother is proud to see him bringing income into the family home and proud that he is 'a worker'.

2.6 For others, stereotypical assumptions – whether based on family, gender, disability or race – seem to limit the type of opportunities that are presented to them. Often these young people, such as Sabrina, Susan and Alan, below, seem to present no obvious 'problem' to society and so their disengagement can go unnoticed and unaddressed.

> ### *Sabrina*
>
> Sabrina is 14 and the eldest child of four. Her mother is a single parent and there are three different fathers to the children. The family as a whole relies heavily on their grandfather, who lives nearby. Sabrina cares for her three brothers when her mother is out of the house; the youngest of whom is 18 months old. Her mother does not work and has a growing drink problem. Social services have visited the home.
>
> Sabrina has a major role in supporting her mother and brothers. The family relies on her; there seems to be an expectation that she will continue to remain at home to assist with keeping the household together. This expectation – which seems to be implicitly shared by the statutory services and the local community – is limiting her opportunities educationally and socially, and in the future will determine her social, career and lifestyle choices. Sabrina will never reach her full potential. She has no clear identified route after 16 for getting her own place or making plans for her own life.

Susan

Susan is now 18. She has lived with her grandmother since she was a baby, when her mother had an accident and fractured her spine. Susan has been caring for her grandmother since the age of nine. Her grandmother is in her eighties and has very limited mobility and some other health problems, and requires full care. Susan makes all her meals, does her shopping each week, cleans her house, does washing and ironing, bathes her once a week, and is 'on call' during the evening in case she requires any help. She also collects her pension and takes care of bills and paperwork. Before her grandmother was offered home care, Susan also washed and dressed her every day.

Susan now attends college full time. When she left school at the age of 16, having missed most of her final year in school as a result of caring for her grandmother, she became a full-time carer, but did not initially receive any state financial support as she was unaware of its existence. Following assessment of her and her grandmother's needs she did receive some benefits but is not longer entitled to them as the course she is studying is considered to be full-time.

Susan and her grandmother had received no help or support until about 18 months ago when they were both assessed by social services. This was the result of a chance visit by a nurse who was dropping off some medical supplies following her grandmother's return home from a spell in hospital. The nurse contacted social services and, following assessment, home care was arranged for 15 minutes in the mornings (Monday to Friday) to get her grandmother up, washed and dressed and an additional hour during the week to help with the washing. The same nurse also put Susan in contact with a young carers project.

Alan

Alan became disabled at 13 as the result of a road accident which left him paralysed.

Until then he had progressed well at school, but as he spent a considerable period of time in a hospital away from his home town, this led to him quickly becoming disengaged from school life and his circle of friends. It also put considerable pressure on his family.

After leaving hospital, Alan was able to return to his mainstream school after adaptations made it accessible to wheelchair users. However, he found it hard to adjust to his disability, as did his friends. As a result he found himself bullied and isolated.

He also felt unable to access the full range of formal, as well as informal, learning opportunities. Inflexible transport provision and a lack of additional support meant that he was unable to attend many of the extra-curricular activities. He was also unable to participate in work experience and to go on some school trips.

Lacking confidence in himself and his own abilities, Alan left school at 16 with no qualifications. He now lives with his family and is socially isolated. He does not feel he has always been well served by professionals such as social workers and occupational therapists, and has not therefore made contact with the Employment Service or other support agencies.

Alan's situation has caused considerable strain on his family. His parents have separated on a number of occasions, citing the stress of their son's disability as the main cause.

Alan, now 19, admits to experiencing spells of severe depression and is very lonely.

2.7 Experience of school is often crucial in shaping a young person's future. For the vast majority, school provides the support and guidance that will allow them to achieve their full potential. But for some, beginning at a new school is a frightening experience that triggers long-term problems.

Emma

Emma, now 19, came from a close family and got on well with both her parents.

But her early life was marked by a series of family moves, leading to her being transferred from school to school. Every time she changed school she worried about making new friends. She decided that to be in with the 'hard' group, she had to behave in a similar way to them. So she became violent to those around her.

Her violent behaviour began with beating up another girl at primary school because she was jealous of the girl coming from a family that was financially better off. She was due to leave the school as her family was moving to a larger house; as a consequence of this incident she was asked not to complete her final weeks.

Emma found the move from primary to secondary school particularly difficult. She 'hated' the teachers and turned her violence on them. Emma's violence also extended outside of school and she had once been charged with actual bodily harm. After two temporary exclusions she was finally excluded permanently.

Emma had been involved in drinking and crime from about 14 onwards. She had begun smoking cannabis at 13 but did not progress to more serious drugs.

Emma was sent to a school for children with behavioural problems. Although she made considerable progress at her new school, and felt that the teachers were helpful and supportive, after six months Emma decided to leave. The friends she had made at the school were leaving and new people would be arriving. Emma admits she was afraid of change and so decided to leave.

2.8 But it is not all gloom. Even where family and other problems seem to point to a future marked by underachievement and social exclusion, intervention at the right time and in the right way can make all the difference between a young person just surviving or being able to thrive and develop. Just what that intervention is depends entirely on the needs and priorities of the individual. Sometimes it can simply be giving the young person 'time out' from the stresses of their situation.

Paul

Paul, now 17, was told to leave home by his parents as a result of conflict that had arisen over his previous non-attendance at school and then his disengagement from any form of education, training or employment. Paul was not at physical risk at home, but the fact that he was unable to make a financial contribution to the household led his parents to kick him out.

He contacted the local Youth Homelessness Unit, which attempted to negotiate a return to the family home. Paul's 'inactivity' and his failure to do something useful with his time was a real issue for his family however, and they were not willing to have him back under these circumstances. Paul was accordingly placed into temporary accommodation.

The social worker attached to the Unit got Paul onto benefit and worked with him, in partnership with the Careers Service, to identify training or employment opportunities. As a result, he took up a gardening apprenticeship, which he really enjoyed and which he attended regularly.

Paul subsequently put in an application with the Unit for supported housing.

However, in the meantime, contact with Paul's family had been maintained. His family was impressed by his commitment to the training he was undertaking, and he has now returned home temporarily on the understanding that he continues to attend regularly. This arrangement is working well.

When Paul moves into his flat it will be with the support of his family

2.9 In other cases, it can simply involve finding ways in which the young person can build self-esteem and confidence by channelling their skills and experience into a project or back into the local community.

Saheer

Saheer, now 22, said that he felt like a stranger in his 600-pupil inner city school, and was unable to turn to any of the teachers for help. He got into trouble several times for 'being disruptive'. Although he did try, taking school work home with him, the atmosphere at home didn't allow him to study. His family wasn't supportive about the need for education or qualifications and so it became easy for him from the age of 14 not to go to school at all.

This, together with his continued poor behaviour, led him to be expelled at 15. He went through long periods of unemployment before working as a porter in a kitchen – paid £40 for a 78-hour week.

But his prospects were turned around when he was encouraged by a youth worker to join a local young people's initiative. He now works as a mentor to disadvantaged Asian children. The young people he works with can relate to him because he has grown up in the same area and gone through the same problems. He feels he also has a credibility that professionals do not share. He says that the sense of achievement he gets from his work comes from knowing he has made a difference to other young people's lives.

He hopes to begin a university degree course next year that will qualify him to continue in youth work.

2.10 Or intervention can involve innovative approaches that attempt to deal with an entire group's problems and needs.

The Brown family

A group of about a dozen boys aged eight to 14, who were part of an extended family, were running riot on their local estate. They were causing a huge amount of damage through vandalism, as well as engaging in shoplifting. Their activities were costing the community thousands of pounds in community safety, housing turnover and negative publicity.

A multi-agency response was made to the problem, with a number of partners working locally with the group.

At first, the problems seemed to get worse, with the young people 'testing' the agencies' resolve. The agencies initially wooed the boys with enticements to greater involvement. The group took advantage of these, which intentionally involved little challenging of their behaviour.

Gradually, however, progress began to be made. The young people became involved in alternatives to their anti-social behaviour. The group has now, almost as a single entity, won the local junior football league, completed Prince's Trust Awards and carried out arts projects.

Part II – The response so far

Chapter 3: What's already happening

This chapter looks at how well the PAT thinks existing policies and services work for young people at risk.

The PAT recognises that a range of new initiatives, some of which have only just been implemented or have still to take effect, have been put in place to tackle current shortcomings.

However, the PAT suggests there is more to be done so that:

- **there is more emphasis on prevention, particularly through work with families;**
- **services are delivered in ways that recognise the specific needs, circumstances and aspirations of disadvantaged young people; and**
- **services are provided wherever they are needed and to all who need them, not haphazardly or on a restricted basis. This is particularly relevant to housing, health, leisure, the education of offenders, benefits and volunteering.**

The policy context

3.1 A broad range of Government services and policies are targeted on tackling and preventing the problems described in **Chapters 1** and **2**.

3.2 Many of these policies have been fundamentally reshaped since this Government took office. The PAT recognises that an ambitious programme of change is already in place or in prospect, the key features of which are set out in **Annex F**.

What is missing?

3.3 Clearly there will be a time lag between the framing of new policies in Whitehall and when people on the ground see a difference. But when they do take effect, they will meet many of the concerns expressed by those whom the PAT visited and heard from in consultation.

3.4 Undoubtedly, however, some of the issues that the PAT has identified are ones where it is less clear that a solution is at hand. Some proposed initiatives may not cover all aspects of the problem as fully as may be necessary. And above all of this, there is no clear strategy or framework into which all of these new policies and approaches fit. The sections that follow consider this in more detail.

Education

3.5 Education represents the cornerstone of the Government's policies on young people. It has the potential to have a huge positive impact on young people at risk, because:

- low achievement and non-attendance at school are key factors for later problems;[65] and
- high expectations, strong relationships with teachers, praise and recognition, and parental interest in education are all key protective factors.[66]

3.6 This is an area that has benefited from a broad range of policy development over the last two years, through the Government's Standards agenda, measures to improve school performance, the National Literacy and Numeracy Strategies, and the reforms of teacher training and teacher pay.

3.7 The SEU reports on *Truancy and School Exclusion*,[67] *Bridging the Gap*[68] and *Teenage Pregnancy*[69] are being implemented and should have a significant impact on attendance, achievement and participation. In addition, PAT 11 on 'Schools Plus' has looked at how schools can be used as a focus for other community services and how the learning of children in deprived communities can be supported.

3.8 These are important changes but the PAT believes that they must be kept under review and judged by their effectiveness in addressing the underachievement of vulnerable groups such as:

- young people from poor backgrounds;
- young people with Special Educational Needs;
- young people from ethnic minority communities; and
- young people in the care system.

3.9 The PAT saw considerable evidence of how far there is to go before these aims are fully achieved on the ground, as the following quotes from responses to its consultation with practitioners and from 'reality-checking' exercises demonstrate.

> *"I was getting bored with the lessons. I knew I couldn't do any work because I couldn't read off the blackboard or stuff like that. And it was always too fast, I just thought 'Right, I can't be bothered with it, I'll just go and get stoned somewhere'."*
>
> BMRB Focus Group work[70]
>
> *"The teachers will ask the bright kids what they want to do. If you're not in the top set they don't concentrate on you."*
>
> Reality Check, Liverpool
>
> *"I wasn't thick, I just needed help."*
>
> Reality Check, Feltham YOI
>
> *"I didn't like history because there was no black history, only cotton fields. They told us about the Saxons and the Romans."*
> *"They don't give you drugs awareness until it's too late, until Year 11, when they say, 'This is cannabis' and we all say, 'Yeah, we know'."*
>
> Real Deal[71]

Families

3.10 Alongside education, the experience of family life is the other highly significant influence on young people's chance of success or failure in later life. As **Chapter 1** recorded:

- family poverty and unemployment, conflict, poor parenting or experience of the care system are all key risk factors for later problems; but
- on the other hand, strong relationships with parents, high expectations, role models, active involvement in families and parental interest in education are all strong protective factors.

3.11 The Government has now set the ambitious goal of ending child poverty in 20 years, and halving it in ten. Since coming to office, it has introduced policies that should improve family income and employment prospects for the most disadvantaged, including increases in Child Benefit, the Working Families' Tax Credit, the National Childcare Strategy, and action on employment, including the New Deal for Lone Parents. The PAT on Jobs (PAT 1)[72] has also produced an impressive package of recommendations.

3.12 The PAT believes that Government policies are increasingly recognising that supporting families is about much more than jobs and income, or even schools. For that reason, the PAT focused more on the challenge of supporting parenting.

3.13 Many say they would welcome more support. The response to the Government's consultation paper *Supporting Families*[73] showed this clearly. Preliminary findings from a separate survey of 2,000 parents in poor neighbourhoods show that no less than two-thirds said that they would like more information about parenting and about half would like help or support at least sometimes.[74]

3.14 The most common requests were for advice and support on:

- what to expect in terms of 'normal' behaviour at different ages;
- how to deal with problematic behaviour;
- advice on matters relating to their child's education;
- the pros and cons of different ways of disciplining their children;
- how to parent teenagers;
- how to talk to their children about growing up, their bodies and sex;
- how to deal with sibling rivalry; and
- how children learn.[75]

3.15 The Government has introduced new policies to tackle some of these needs. The most significant step has probably been the development of the Sure Start programme. This programme aims to work with parents and children to promote the physical, intellectual and social development of pre-school children.[76] It builds on models in other countries which have demonstrated success in getting children ready to learn by the time compulsory schooling starts and reducing the incidence of problems such as school drop-out, unemployment, welfare dependency and offending in later life.

3.16 However, Sure Start is still only in its early stages and current plans will see it extending to cover only seven per cent of the population by 2001. The programme is being reviewed in the current Spending Review.

3.17 For older children, provision is much patchier. While parents of babies and toddlers often seek out both preparation for parenthood and later support, for older children and teenagers, seeking information, advice or mediation is perceived to be unusual.

3.18 The Home Office (HO) has set up a three-year programme called On Track, a £30 million project operating in 20 to 25 areas. This is a programme targeted at primary school age children and their families, to prevent offending at age ten and above. Through their Family Support Grants they provide small amounts (total budget is £7 million over three years) to innovative projects. The National Family and Parenting Institute, and National Parent Helpline[77] are also now in existence.

3.19 At local level, there are a few pioneering family support schemes, particularly parenting programmes, which are beginning to address the needs of young people and their families. Many of these are run by the voluntary sector, albeit that their funding often comes from local social services departments.

3.20 However, in many areas family support is not available or is inadequate:

- **crisis-oriented**: there is a lack of preventive support such as family mediation or respite care. As one young person said in the Real Deal consultation project, "There needs to be a total family breakdown before they'll help you.";[78]

- **family support is not always in a form all parents feel comfortable with**: for instance, it may be delivered through social services which some parents associate with child protection and 'problem families' (although some social services departments have managed to overcome this by contracting with local voluntary sector groups). It may require families to make their way to a family centre, rather than receive support in their home. Or some groups, such as those from ethnic minority backgrounds, may feel excluded from what is provided because its delivery is not sufficiently sensitive to their particular needs and priorities;[79]

- **inflexible**: statutory services may not shape their provision around the needs of individual families. As one social worker said of a local voluntary project in Derbyshire, "They can be so much more flexible than we can. They can go shopping, find accommodation, look through the paper with them for jobs, help filling in application forms. Whatever is necessary.";[80] and

- even more flexibility is needed in situations where **teenagers and parents have very different needs and may need separate sources of help.**

> *"There are few services for young people affected by family conflict and this is much needed. In one area, over 2,500 per month call a help line provided via the local authority and most calls are about this issue."*
>
> Somerset County Council Youth Service
>
> *"My 18 year old daughter, she was really good, full of fun, a really happy child, but from the age of 11 she became a woman overnight. It was really difficult, she just wanted to go out with her friends. She really felt she was 16 or 17. That was a really difficult stage, really rebellious, it was an instant thing... I just couldn't seem to cope with... it was really frightening."*
>
> *"I think there should be parenting sessions, where they tell you how to deal with it when a child's doing this, what you should actually do, for example, when they blackmail you into giving them things. I've always given in too easily, because I've always thought that she's going to leave, she's going to walk out."*
>
> BMRB Focus Group work
>
> *"I couldn't cope with my mum's drinking any more. I couldn't cope with the bullying."*
>
> *"[What's needed is] some sort of counselling – maybe where families can go and sort out stuff and stop arguing."*
>
> *"The way that they resolve a dispute... is usually a shout, a scream, a violent argument and very often a thump."*
>
> *Still Running*[81]

3.21 More analysis of these issues is set out in **Annex D**, and family support is a key theme in the proposals in **Chapter 9**.

Youth support

> *"I think all the help I need is people telling me that I can do it. I mean, 'You can do it.'"*
>
> *"Help I need? I need a lot of support. I need a lot of guidance. Sometimes, I might just need a little shoulder to cry on sometimes, know what I mean, and they say that men don't cry but that's a load of rubbish to be quite honest."*
>
> Callum, 24, Real Deal

3.22 In its visits and consultations the PAT faced many representations about the need for high-quality **practical and emotional support** for young people. Many young people feel that this is not provided by their families. As one person said, *"Well, I don't really get support, I had to learn from quite young to be able to deal with things like that."*

3.23 Particular issues repeatedly raised were:

- the need for more consistent coverage and provision for the **Youth Service** – funding, provision and effectiveness are very patchy;[82] and
- the importance of high-quality **careers advice** and support for the most disadvantaged young people before and after the age of 16.

3.24 The Government has accepted the force of these arguments and has put forward an ambitious commitment to develop a new universal youth support service, the Connexions Service.[83] This will provide personal advice and support to all young people and will work closely with other specialist services. It has been envisaged almost as the equivalent of a 'GP service' in the health field, where personal advisers would be able to provide some non-specialist help themselves as well as refer on to other services and follow up those who have had more specialist help. It will ensure services combine to meet the needs of the individual.

3.25 The Connexions Service clearly represents the major policy development in this field for the foreseeable future, and the PAT believes it represents a huge opportunity to improve the quality and co-ordination of support for young people. But the critical challenges for implementation and further development will be to ensure that:

- the Service meshes effectively with other local players, and in particular with local authority mainstream services;
- new professional structures and methods are developed for those working in the Service; and
- the specialist services to which young people may need to be referred are available and suitable.

3.26 Ensuring that suitable specialist services, to whom young people can be referred, are available, is particularly relevant to the points made below on specialist health services and policies towards offenders.

Mental and physical health services

3.27 Concern about the adequacy and suitability of key specialist health services for young people was a repeated theme of the PAT's visits and consultations.

Mental health services

3.28 Access to, and quality of, **mental health services** were a particular concern for many. The problems highlighted in the Audit Commission's report, *Children in Mind*,[84] and the PAT's consultations were:

- **a mismatch between needs and resources**: spending on Child and Adolescent Mental Health Services (CAMHS) per head of the local child population was found to vary by a factor of seven. One in ten services could not offer a first appointment for non-urgent cases within six months. Many of the services were not organised on the basis of a coherent assessment of need;
- **a postcode lottery**: inconsistency in terms of the professional mix of staff and the kind of interventions offered. As the Audit Commission's report says, "Children with similar problems were seen by different professions in different trusts... referrals may sometimes be allocated on the basis of which professionals had the time available, rather than on their particular skills";
- **a shortage of skilled professionals** and a lack of training and support for others who could play a part in dealing with mental health problems;
- lack of clarity over the **age range** of services: one in five health authorities are said to be unclear about the age ranges covered by their services. One in three commission services for children up to the age of 16 only. In addition to these, in many places the transition from children's to adults' services is disjointed and lacks co-ordination; and

- **lack of mental health services for offenders**: 75 per cent of young people convicted of the most serious and violent offences have themselves been victims of physical, sexual or emotional abuse[85] and therefore potentially suffer mental health problems as a result. There are, however, only 16 NHS secure mental health care beds for young people in the whole country[86] and too many young people with mental health problems end up, untreated, in custody.

3.29 The Government is already starting to respond to some of these problems. The *National Priorities Guidance for 1999–2002*, jointly issued to the NHS and social services, included a joint health and social care objective for CAMHS. A total of £90 million has been set aside to build up and improve locally-based CAMHS over this three-year period.

3.30 The commitment to improving CAMHS throughout the country is of particular relevance to young people who experience, or are at risk of, social exclusion. But it will require shortfalls in staffing levels and training provision to be addressed, as well as the development of new approaches to reaching young people with mental health problems, if the needs of those who are unable or reluctant to access existing services are to be fully met.

> *"Because I had bottled so much up over the years, it was difficult for me to express how I felt and sort of where to start. I went to see a psychiatrist. I went there for a year and all I did was sit there and look at the clock. The way he was trying to get things out of me was the wrong way of doing it because I was very young."*
>
> *"Here, sensibly, you have to be pretty bad to be taken on by the mental health team and that's right because you don't want to be labelling people when it's not right to be doing that."*
>
> *Still Running*
>
> *"Luck seems to play far too great a part in receiving good service – living in the right place at the right time, having a knowledgeable and helpful GP, having able social workers, having local services that co-operate with one another – all these seem to depend on luck."*
>
> *Bright Futures*[87]

Sexual health and advice services

3.31 The SEU's *Teenage Pregnancy*[88] report showed how the shortage of appropriate **sexual health and advice services** was one factor in this country's low rates of contraceptive use and high rates of teenage pregnancy and sexually transmitted diseases. Issues included: location and opening hours of advice services; lack of advertising and information; young people's concern about confidentiality; a belief that services are designed for adults and those in stable relationships; and young men and people from ethnic minorities often feel particularly excluded.

3.32 In addition, the report highlighted: a severe lack of local co-ordination among all the services involved; a failure to maximise the preventive potential of education; and a failure to involve the voluntary sector, parents and young people themselves.

3.33 Delivering improved service co-ordination, prevention and contraception services, and supporting schools and parents in providing better sex education, are now key elements in delivering the Government's aims to halve the number of under-18 conceptions over ten years as well as its broader sexual health goals.

Drugs and alcohol education, advice and treatment

3.34 **Chapter 1** set out the worrying levels of drug and alcohol use among young people. A number of Government initiatives are aimed at this.

3.35 The first of four main aims of the ten-year Drugs Strategy[89] is helping young people resist drug misuse in order to achieve their full potential in society. As part of this work, data on the prevalence of drug misuse by young people aged under 25 will be gathered every two years, allowing trends to be more accurately assessed. The Green Paper *Our Healthier Nation*[90] also announced the preparation of a new strategy on alcohol, and a forthcoming White Paper on liquor licensing will cover controls intended to tackle under-age drinking.

3.36 These are important developments and ensuring that they have adequate coverage and effective answers for young people is essential. Any policies developed need to meet the concerns widely encountered by this PAT in its visits and consultations.

- The availability of what support there is, is inconsistent from place to place. One area where considerable improvements *have* been made is in the provision of drug treatment services for young people in custody. Unfortunately, such improvements have not been replicated in community services.
- Services fail to reach many young people with drug or alcohol problems. For instance, a survey of prisoners under the age of 18 showed that three-quarters of those who admitted to having a current or previous drink problem had never received any help with their problems. They can easily fall through the net both of general health and specialist drug services.
- Drugs education by schools across the country is fragmented and variable in quality. Not all schools operate policies in drug education, in line with Department for Education and Employment (DfEE) guidelines.
- There is no specific Government programme aimed at tackling the use of Class A drugs by those aged 16 or under.

Crime and victimisation

Tackling youth crime

3.37 Since coming to office, the Government has embarked on major changes in the way youth offending is dealt with. The youth justice provisions of the Crime and Disorder Act, 1998 provide the platform for this, through new powers for the police and the courts, and new, multi-disciplinary structures at local and national level. YOTs, which will be introduced nationally from April 2000, will bring together for the first time all the key local agencies with a contribution to make to reducing youth offending – police, social services, education, probation and health, with the scope to involve others, including the voluntary sector.

3.38 The intent behind the Act was both to prevent and tackle youth offending. There is, however, a recognition that in their early stages of development, and before they go on a nationwide footing, the YOTs have concentrated almost exclusively on the crisis intervention aspects of their work. There is also some evidence[91] that, perhaps due to this lack of preventive focus, there have been difficulties in engaging partners from the health and education sectors fully in the work of the YOTs.

Victimisation

3.39 Young people are more likely to be *victims* of crime than any other section of society.[92] A recurrent theme among surveys of young people is the fear of bullying and crime, particularly violent crime. In some places these concerns are expressed through a fear of travel, and increased 'territoriality'. In others, there is the additional factor of the very real fear of racial harassment and violence.

3.40 Many young people feel that the police automatically see them as the problem, assuming they will be the potential perpetrators of crime rather than its most likely victims. This perception is particularly strong among young people from ethnic minorities, and the Macpherson report[93] has illustrated the problems that underpin this.

3.41 There are good examples of community liaison with young people by the police, and of schemes designed to break down barriers. But these have not been established on a consistent basis across the country, and often have to rely on the goodwill or initiative of individual officers and on temporary sources of funding.

Rehabilitating offenders

3.42 Poor skills are known to increase the risk of reoffending, yet education and training has traditionally been a low priority in prison.

3.43 A criminal record is also a barrier to employment. Thirteen per cent of young people aged 16–17 not in education, training or employment mentioned a criminal record as a barrier to employment.

3.44 The SEU's report *Bridging the Gap* committed the Government to improving education for offenders and the co-ordinated handling of education issues for offenders, through:

- 30 hours' education and personal development per week for offenders aged 17 or younger;
- better ways of assessing educational needs;
- better co-ordination between YOTs, personal advisers, and whoever is responsible when in custody; and
- ensuring an education or training place is available for each young offender before release.

Leaving home: housing and benefits and financial support

> *"I knew she [mum] was going to throw me out some day because the same thing happened to my big sisters when they were 16 or 17. It was still unexpected. Now she keeps threatening to my brother and sister that they are the next to go."*
>
> *"I'm staying round friends' houses at the moment. Quite a few friends really. It has been like this for two months now. I had a flat. I had a lot of trouble up there because I was young and living on my own. I had a lot of break-ins and my nerves were so bad I had to get out. So I've just been staying around here."*
>
> *Still Running*

3.45 As the case studies in **Chapter 2** show, some young people are catapulted out of their home while still in their teens by arguments, family break-up, poverty and abuse. For these young people, the safety net is failing. This is particularly true for those struggling to overcome trauma and disadvantage, and for those suffering mental health problems, poor skills and unemployment.

> *"A Citizen's Advice Bureau in Essex reported a 17 year old who was pregnant and homeless. Her parents refused to allow her home... she was surviving on £15 a week bridging allowance, was unable to find anywhere to live and had been refused severe hardship."*
>
> *Sort it out!*[94]
>
> *"There are so many rules and hoops that they [young people] have to jump through now as well. In terms of their initial contact of making a claim, they now have to prove their identity... not many young people have a driver's licence, passport or birth certificate, especially if they're homeless and that age range (16 to 17). Trying to get a birth certificate means having contact with the family that they don't want to have contact with."*
>
> *Still Running*
>
> *"They [DSS/JobCentre] don't tell you everything you need to know... you need to find out for yourself and go back and tell* ***them****!"*
>
> Reality Check, Hull

Housing

3.46 In many parts of the country, there is a **lack of good-quality affordable housing**. The reasons for this are complex. They include:

- rising rents because of demographic pressures, for example in London;
- reduced access to social housing as a consequence of Right to Buy;
- physical disrepair, and location in areas of high crime and vandalism; and
- lack of an integrated housing strategy in many areas. This consists of needs assessment, audit of services and planning of provision to meet young people's needs.

3.47 Access to affordable housing is limited because of the lack of priority given to young people's housing needs. The forthcoming revised Homelessness Code of Guidance addresses this up to a point.[95] However, homeless young people are still not automatically considered to be in priority need. The Single Room Rent Restriction applied to Housing Benefit may also restrict young people's choice: a limited research study suggests that in some areas, very little accommodation is available within what Housing Benefit will pay for for those single young people aged under 25.[96]

3.48 Young people are often shunted between housing and social services with neither department taking responsibility. While in some areas successful Housing Act/Children Act joint protocols operate, in many areas there is a lack of co-ordination between departments.

3.49 Young people do better if they get support from independent advocacy and advice agencies. But these are scarce and many young people are unaware of them.

3.50 As part of the Youth Homelessness Action Partnership (YHAP), the Department of the Environment, Transport and the Regions (DETR) has commissioned two research projects. These are attempting to:

- bring together what is currently known about the nature and causes of homelessness among young people, and provide an estimate of the numbers affected, broken down by age, gender, ethnic background and other factors; and
- establish a database of current initiatives aimed at tackling and preventing youth homelessness. Evaluation of a range of projects will inform production of a guide to good practice.

Benefits

3.51 One of the most powerful messages that emerges from consulting young people is that the benefits system as it operates offers inadequate protection, particularly for those who have left home under 18. As described in the SEU's *Bridging the Gap* report, support for under-18s is delivered through a variety of benefits and allowances, administered by different agencies from different locations. The complexity of the system and the confusion over the terms and conditions prevent many young people getting the help they need.

3.52 On the basis of the PAT's work, attention is drawn specifically to the problems connected with proving eligibility for Jobseeker's Allowance (JSA) Severe Hardship Payments and Income Support. Agencies working with homeless and other very vulnerable young people find commonly that:

- young people often do not know what they may be entitled to;
- they find it difficult to navigate their way through the steps involved (with the Careers Service and the Employment Service);
- they may face poor practice and insensitivity from staff; and
- their case may involve a requirement to prove estrangement – this is problematic for young people and difficult for the agencies involved to administer.

Leaving care

3.53 For young people in and leaving care, there are particular problems. The Utting Report[97] showed how the existing arrangements were failing this most vulnerable group of young people.

- As many as 75 per cent of care leavers have no GCSEs, compared with six per cent of all school leavers.
- Up to 20 per cent of care leavers experience some form of homelessness within two years of leaving care.
- Up to 50 per cent of care leavers are unemployed.
- There is an increasing trend for local authorities to discharge young people from care early, largely for financial reasons. The proportion leaving care at the age of 16 increased from 33 per cent in 1993, to 46 per cent (3,600) in 1998. This is in contrast to the average for the population as a whole, where young people typically leave home at 22.
- Too many young people experience very little support upon leaving care, both in terms of financial help and advice and guidance.
- Young people leaving care move into a variety of accommodation. While some of this is suitable and good quality, for example supported lodgings, too much is not, for example B&B or accommodation in unsafe or unsuitable areas.

3.54 The Government has made a start in tackling the problems of young people in the transition to independence, including:

- the forthcoming revision of the DETR *Code of Guidance for Local Authorities on the Allocation of Accommodation and Homelessness,* currently in draft, which recommends that local authorities consider all young care leavers as vulnerable under the homelessness legislation;
- Quality Protects, improving the management and effectiveness of local authority social services for children; and
- a range of measures, detailed in the Department of Health (DH) document *Me? Survive? Out there?,*[98] to improve services for care leavers, to reduce their risk of social exclusion and ensure they are able to participate socially and economically as citizens.

Community participation and leisure

3.55 Several initiatives to improve leisure and community participation opportunities for young people have been announced:

- the New Audiences Programme, encouraging young people to participate in the arts;
- the Youth Card, to support access to leisure by providing discounts for publicly- and privately-owned facilities; and
- the Millennium Volunteers initiative, to promote and recognise voluntary activity by young people aged 16–25.

3.56 The Government's forthcoming Sports Strategy will also pay particular attention to the need to encourage greater participation by young people in physical recreation.

3.57 The PAT welcomes these initiatives but they do not guarantee that all young people will have access to the full range of opportunities. Leisure and the opportunity to contribute constructively to the community are important to young people. Their lack of access can lead to much more risky activities such as drugs, sex and crime. The PAT considers that this needs to be reflected in Government priorities.

3.58 There is much evidence from successful good practice that participation in voluntary and community activity can benefit both young people themselves and their communities. They learn and develop as individuals, as well as providing a valuable service to others. Millennium Volunteers and other Government programmes are in place to promote voluntary and community activity, and the SEU's *Bridging the Gap* report drew attention to the potential for this kind of activity both to deliver better youth support and as a component of the 'graduation' concept. However, the availability of opportunities remains very patchy and awareness is low. There is also an issue whether such opportunities will prove effective in attracting the interest and involvement of the most disengaged young people.

3.59 In all the PAT's visits and discussions with young people, the lack of safe, interesting and affordable leisure facilities emerged as a huge issue. A strong theme was that young people were criticised for hanging around, or amusing themselves in disruptive ways, when there were no high-quality alternatives on offer.

3.60 Where good facilities do exist, cost, location and transport were cited as severe obstacles to participation. As one young person said, *"They are too expensive, too far to travel to and that costs money too."*[99]

3.61 For disabled young people, the physical barriers are even worse. For example, people living in the poorest areas are more reliant on public transport, which is still largely inaccessible to disabled people with mobility problems. Indeed, it will be another 20 years before all mainstream buses are fully accessible.

3.62 Leisure facilities for young people are not always available in the right form across the whole age range. Youth service provision, for example, does not always cater effectively for the needs of older young people. As a young person said, *"People have nothing to do when you're too old for the youth clubs, and that's at 13 or 14, and then it's just the pub. There's nothing else to do. There's a big gap."*[100]

3.63 The action the PAT believes is necessary to improve the services is set out in **Chapter 10**.

Chapter 4: Does Government spend more on deprived young people?

This chapter questions whether public services spend more on children and young people living in deprived areas. Information is patchy because Government does not routinely measure what it spends on particular groups of people. However, recent research reveals that while Government spending on children generally increases with increasing deprivation, there are a number of instances where children living in very deprived wards have less spent on them than those in more affluent ones. Furthermore, emerging evidence suggests that on average, the state spends 14 per cent less money on young people in the most deprived areas than on the average young person.

4.1 **Chapter 3** showed that many services for young people are failing to meet young people's needs. One of the consistent messages from the PAT's consultation was that while spending on young people in general was increasing, some services simply needed more resources.

4.2 The conventional wisdom is that the Government targets more money to deprived areas, families and individuals than it does to more affluent areas, therefore it needs to focus more on how the money is spent rather than its overall level.

4.3 This assumption has been difficult to test because of a lack of information. Government does not routinely analyse how much total spending on all services is directed towards particular areas or groups.

4.4 However, a recent study[101] has provided some insight into the relationship between spending and deprivation.

4.5 The research shows that:

- looking at Government spending for all ages, more is spent on deprived areas than non-deprived. But there are anomalies. Although wards with *very* high levels of deprivation often had high spending, those which are only slightly less deprived often had less money than the more affluent wards; however,

- for children aged 0–15, the research, and further work undertaken by this PAT, reveals that while Government spending generally seems to increase with increasing deprivation, there are a number of instances where children living in some of the most deprived wards have *less* spent on them than those living in more affluent areas[102] (**Figure 3**).

4.6 One of the reasons why the relationship between spending on children and deprivation is unclear is that **spending seems to take little account of the fact that deprived areas have higher concentrations of children.**

Figure 3: Spending on those aged 0–15 by Index of Local Conditions

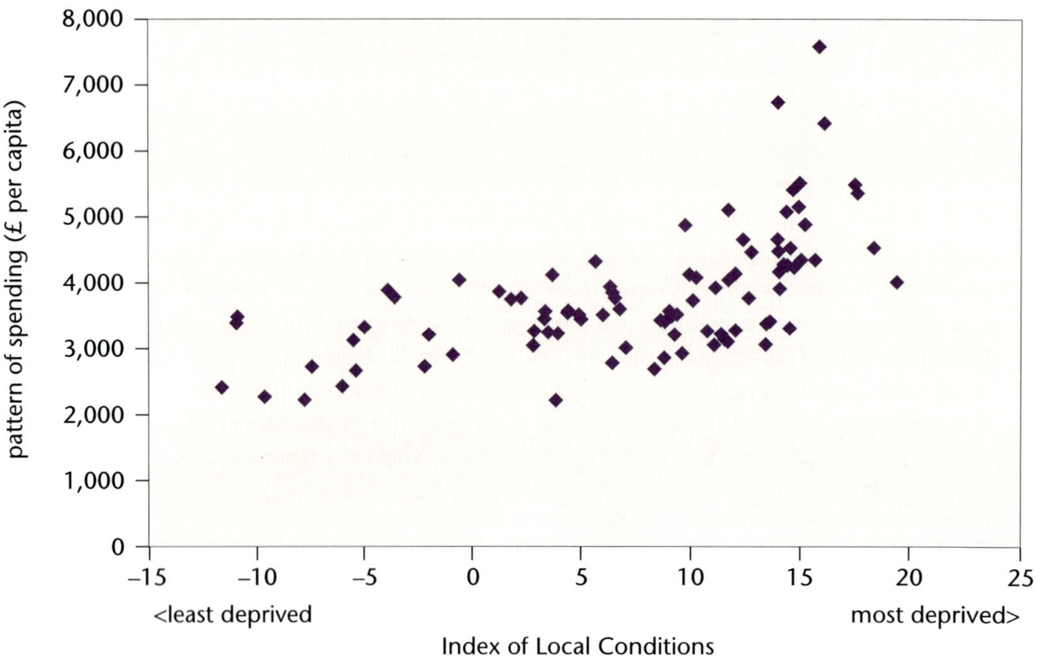

Source: Bramley et al, 1998.

4.7 For young people aged 16 to 24, the pattern of spending seems to differ. Generally, as deprivation increases so spending *decreases*. With the exception of a few of the most deprived wards where expenditure is higher, the researchers suggested that spending on young people living in the most deprived areas amounted to some **14 per cent less** than the average.[103] The main explanation for this imbalance is the money spent on further and higher education.

Policy implications

4.8 The research on public spending has two main implications:

- the assumption that we spend more on our poorest young people seems to be wrong.[104] Given the need to tackle the roots of social exclusion, the PAT believes the Government should consider how it can **redirect spending towards the most deprived areas and individuals.** In particular, spending needs to account for the higher concentrations of children and young people in poor areas; and

- the urgent need for **better information** on funding flows. The researchers had great difficulty in obtaining raw data to carry out the analysis. Information held by local authorities was often inconsistent and incomplete. A long-term aim should be for this kind of information to be available routinely, rather than through special research.

Chapter 5: Coherence

This chapter looks at how the approach of Government to young people at risk looks as a whole. It concludes that there is a big gap, in several dimensions: at national and local level; in the evidence base for policy; and in the lack of machinery for bringing policies and services together. This is not a matter of academic interest or administrative tidiness. It is at the root of many of the issues identified in Chapter 4; it is at the heart of the failure of most services to work preventively; and it leads to young people getting a raw deal.

5.1 The last four chapters paint a gloomy picture. They show that:

- a significant minority of young people in this country face some quite serious problems, many of which have been on a worsening trend;
- for a significant number of these issues, we do worse than many other comparable countries; and
- these problems are concentrated in deprived areas, yet some deprived areas actually get less money to spend on children and young people than their more affluent neighbours.

5.2 Many mainstream services are now addressing the needs of these young people – or planning to. Many of the responses are only available in a minority of areas or are still only in the early stages of development.

5.3 All in all, there is still a long way to go. Why did things get to this state?

5.4 The PAT believes that at the root of these problems lies a structural weakness – the failure of existing structures to provide a coherent national approach to policy on young people at risk. For decades, no-one has had clear responsibility for making this happen, either in central or local government. This has allowed the increased focus on agencies' individual objectives to lead to less focus on the problems that straddle boundaries. Unless this is addressed, delivery and design of new policies may fall short of what the Government wants to achieve; indeed there is a risk that new initiatives could actually add so much confusion that their underlying goals are seriously jeopardised.

5.5 The problem is easily demonstrated by looking at the Policy Map at **Annex F**, which the PAT constructed to illustrate some of the key initiatives addressing young people. This shows that:

- no fewer than eight Government departments and six cross-cutting units have a significant interest in tackling the issues identified in this report;
- many of them are doing so through cross-cutting initiatives but some of these appear to duplicate each other (for example, until recently, DfEE and HO were running quite similar volunteering programmes for young people) and others fall awkwardly between departments (for example, responsibility for parenting and family-based interventions and policing child employment);

- a large number of issues are only being met through initiatives that are short term or limited in geographical coverage – without a strategy for what will happen once they are completed or how needs are to be met in other places;

- many issues are only being tackled by special regeneration programmes, rather than mainstream services; and

- plans and partnerships proliferate – see the box below. These consume huge amounts of senior time at local level – but underlying services remain parallel rather than joined up and the system is poor at tackling young people who have more than one problem. Perhaps more importantly, a young person can find themselves subject to a confusing number of plans.

Plans for children and young people (and their lead Government department)

- Children's Services Plan and Quality Protects (DH)
- Education Development Plan (DfEE)*
- Behaviour Support Plans (DfEE)
- Special Educational Needs Plans (DfEE)
- Early Years and Child Care Development Plans (DfEE)*
- Youth Justice Plans (Youth Justice Board/HO)
- Crime and Disorder Strategies (HO)
- Drug Action Plans (UK Anti-Drugs Co-ordination Unit, Cabinet Office)
- Health Improvement Programmes (DH)*

*denotes universal plans

5.6 The greatest cost is to the vulnerable young people who pass through the hands of countless agencies without the young person's problems ever being tackled effectively. Even while the PAT has been writing this report, the inquiry into the death of a 13 year old girl in London discovered that she had been in contact with some 230 professionals from ten different agencies.

> *"Many young people fall between services that are not geared up to meet their needs – services that often create barriers through ill thought out and unco-ordinated strategies. Most services are compartmentalised and fail to deliver an integrated and holistic service at the point of need."*
>
> The Big Issue in the North
>
> *"I've had loads of social workers and key workers and leaving care scheme workers and what have you, but they eventually leave you alone as well... you know what I mean. They're all enthusiastic in the beginning, 'Oh, I'll help you out with this and that' and then they slowly fade away, lose contact with you."*
>
> *Still Running*
>
> *"Young people need a central and accessible advice and guidance point. The all too frequent situation, where young people have to go from one agency to another to get benefits or services, is very damaging. They often need an advocate to help them manage the process."*
>
> Warwickshire Careers
>
> *"There is a competitive market in funding for services for young people, forcing agencies to bid and tender against one another and guard their interests."*
>
> Consultation with Practitioners

Central government

5.7 The way central government is organised is part of the reason for this confusion. This has a number of mutually reinforcing features:

- **It is no-one's job to ensure coherent design and delivery of Government policies on young people at risk.** No single department is in the lead, and the work that departments undertake individually sometimes overlaps confusingly and leaves gaps. For example, DH is responsible for all children in need up to the age of 18, with the aim of maximising "the social development of children within stable family settings"; DfEE's aims include building skills and personal qualities into children up to the age of 16, and encouraging lifelong learning for all adults; and HO has also recently taken on responsibility for family policy. But none of these could reasonably be described as exercising, or has ever been asked to exercise, a cross-Government leadership role on overall policy on children and young people.

- Added to this, **there is no permanent youth policy cross-Whitehall Ministerial committee or official network.** Work has either been done in ad hoc meetings between departments, summoned together for a single issue, or has been pushed by groups whose primary focus is something else, for example the Ministers for Women and the 'teenage boys' sub-group of the Ministerial Committee on the Family. But there is no machinery to bring together all the strands of policy and to present them as a coherent whole.

- All this means there is **no single point of contact** where people inside and outside Government can go to get or give information. There is no-one to speak (or listen!) to young people for the Government across the whole range of issues affecting them. There is no one place of contact in Whitehall where the voluntary sector, business and people from other countries can deposit and access information about Government policies, research findings and questions, examples of good practice, networks of external and international contacts, or wisdom about how to involve young people in policy dialogue.

- **Inside departments, responsibility is fragmented too.** In many cases, no-one is clearly in the lead and responsible for looking at the impact of all the department's policies on young people. So:

- one bit of a department may be unaware of what another bit is doing, creating scope for duplication and conflicts. Often only Ministers see the whole picture, and that in only a piecemeal way;
- knowledge and networks are often built up, but not sustained and shared, so there is great scope for 'reinventing the wheel';
- cross-Whitehall initiatives find it hard to identify someone who can cover all of a department's interest; and
- individuals who get involved in broader initiatives find they acquire a high burden of internal co-ordination, in addition to their 'day job'.

Local level

5.8 But the problem is not confined to central government:

- The PAT has heard repeatedly from local practitioners that it is almost **impossible to find out about other services or initiatives at local level.** Establishing local information networks appears to be nobody's job.
- **Agreeing joint priorities appears to be just as difficult.** This is exacerbated by the fact that many of the services are the responsibility of different arms of central government or tiers of local government. Three sets of recent developments – the Children's Services Planning process (see box below), specific joining up around particular issues like YOTs and Drug Action Teams (DATs), and the commitment to establish the Connexions Service – are welcome. But in the consultation and in other settings, many people on the ground have suggested that unless the links between these developments are properly thought through they may just add to the confusion. It is important that local authorities consider this as they establish new executive committees and scrutiny arrangements.

Children's Services Planning

Children's Services Planning was made mandatory in March 1996. Plans bring together services for children and young people in need (up to the age of 18, or 21 in the case of those who have been looked after). Local authorities must assess the needs of children in their area, consult a wide range of bodies (including voluntary organisations) in planning how that need should be met, and publish the resulting plans. Guidance issued to local authorities encourages (but cannot legally require) joint planning for the welfare of children generally.

The Government has announced that the guidance will be strengthened by making joint planning a duty of the corporate authority as a whole and requiring other local agencies to contribute. The White Paper *Modernising Social Services*[105] said that in future Children's Services Plans would summarise the intention of all other relevant plans and thus bring together action on behalf of all the main groups of children at the risk of social exclusion.

Guidance is currently being produced by DH which will establish Children's Services Planning as *the* vehicle for consolidating all planning activity which affects the well-being of children and young people.

- Undoubtedly, **local fragmentation is often caused and made worse by fragmented and contradictory interventions from central government**. These include:
  - overlapping or conflicting statutory requirements;
  - the plethora of initiatives and plans (see **Annex F** and the box at paragraph 5.5);
  - funding and priorities that deal with only one dimension of young people's needs rather than the web of issues they may face; and
  - the tendency for policies to be delivered through ad hoc partnerships that are meant to promote innovation and inclusiveness, but – unless rationalised – probably make it even harder to do the delivery and joining up that everyone says they aspire to.
- It does not help that different agencies and initiatives use different geographical boundaries. The map below, prepared by the London Borough of Newham, shows graphically how the overlap of one regeneration initiative with another quickly produces a dizzying mosaic of boundaries.

Overlap of one regeneration initiative with another in the London Borough of Newham

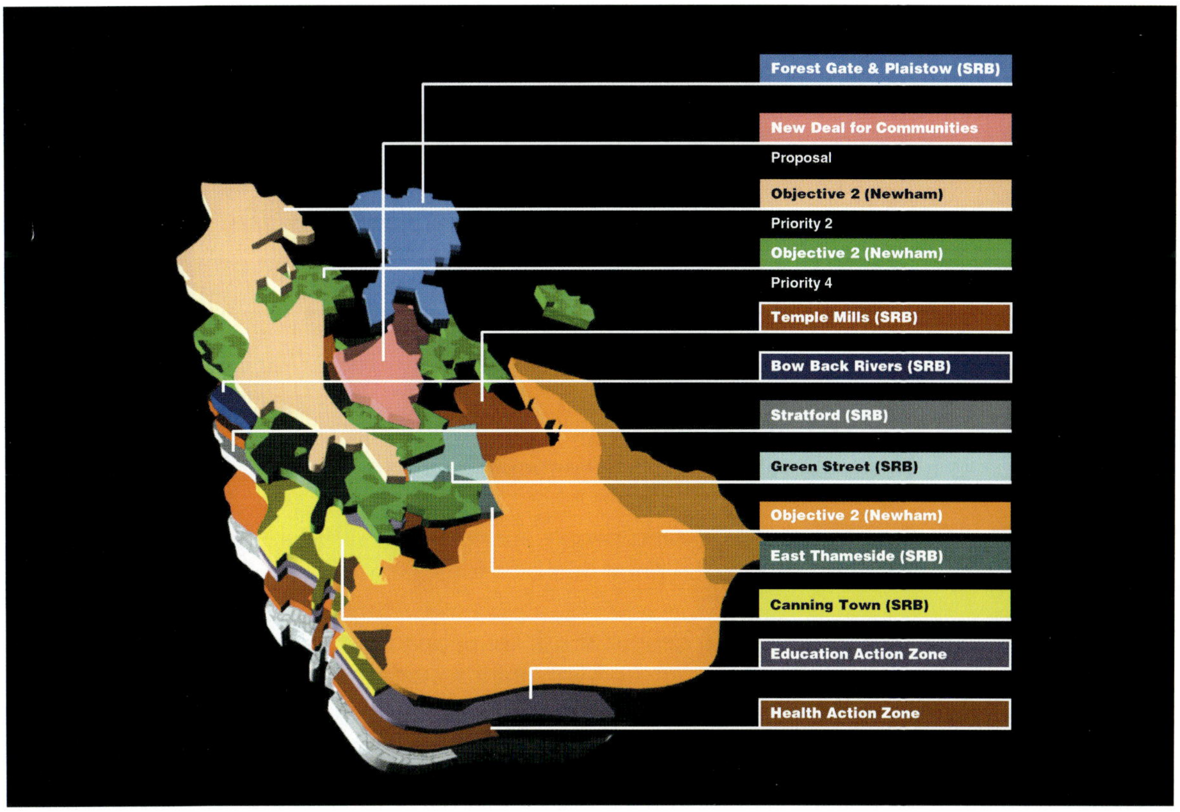

Why poor co-ordination leads to problems

The effect on young people

5.9 The lack of a clear big picture is not a matter of merely academic interest, or of administrative tidiness. **It has a direct impact on the quality of help young people receive and, as a result, on the quality of their lives:**

- **Young people get shunted from agency to agency** because responsibilities are unclear. For instance, young people leaving home at 16 may be passed between housing, social services and the benefits system. As a result, **young people can fall through the cracks in agency responsibilities, and services can appear contradictory, complex and inaccessible.**

- **Young people with multiple risk factors often go without help.** A young person may be 'known to' several agencies but no individual problem is serious enough to merit attention. For instance, as Hertfordshire Young Citizens Programme found, a young person may have truanted from school, had severe family problems and committed crime but may be receiving no support from any agency.[106] By contrast, others may be having to deal with several different professionals in isolation and may be playing different agencies off against each other.

- While the PAT acknowledges that some agencies feel bound by principles of confidentiality, **there is often a problem with the legitimate exchange of information between agencies, resulting in young people receiving a poorer service.** It has been reported that:

  - the Employment Service does not share its information on job opportunities with community centres and other organisations; and

  - information is not always passed on between primary and secondary schools so teachers may be unaware of an individual's particular needs and preferences.

How resources are channelled

5.10 Two very strong messages emerged from the PAT's consultation and visits about the way resources are often channelled into poor neighbourhoods and for young people at risk:

- too often the specific needs of young people are not given sufficient attention in the way regeneration programmes are designed and bids for such funding put together; and

- far too many services for young people at risk are dependent on project funding, administered by a multiplicity of statutory, lottery and voluntary sector schemes, each with its own rules and timescales, and with no guarantee of continuation after a fixed term, however important and effective the service. The salary of one worker in a project visited by the PAT was being met from ten different such sources.

> *"Perhaps the most fundamental difficulty we encounter when we attempt to develop initiatives to tackle social exclusion is that of funding. Our current experience is that all partners are faced with a 'patchwork quilt' of funding resources – Single Regeneration Budget (SRB)/European Social Fund (ESF)/mainstream – all of which have different management and accountability requirements as well as seeking to target differing groups within the 'socially excluded'."*
>
> Bolton and Bury Chamber
>
> *"There is too much short-term finance. Support needs to be in mainstream budgets."*
>
> Burnley College
>
> *"ESF funding is too short term! Short-term funding for training and service providers is a major problem. With two organisations now, we have had short-term contracts due to ESF funding. Both have been helping individual young people into employment or training but both programmes have had to stop when the first year's funding was not renewed. Continued funding for successful up and running projects should take priority over funding new projects."*
>
> Diocesan Youth Service

5.11 Groups working with young people from ethnic minority communities point out that these deficiencies in funding mechanisms bear particularly hard on them, because of their often extreme disadvantage, and because mainstream services cater badly for their needs.

5.12 The deployment of professional resources on young people in poor neighbourhoods does not achieve its full potential because it is not well co-ordinated. In the PAT's consultations and visits many professionals working with young people drew attention to how much more they could achieve with a clearer overall vision and strategy:

> *"With a plethora of initiatives and consultations published covering a variety of policy areas (health, housing, learning, employment), it is not clear to service providers what the Government's holistic strategy for young people is. It would be helpful if Government would adopt a holistic approach to its policy making for young people."*
>
> National Council for Voluntary Youth Services
>
> *"We don't know who's taking ownership of the agenda to combat disengagement and foster re-engagement. The waters are still very muddy – some services are specific to young people, some are general services, but treat young people differently; some make no distinction between young people and older people."*
>
> Consultation with Practitioners
>
> *"In our experience local planning for young people's provision has been most notable for its absence."*
>
> Youth Access

5.13 The lack of focus and strategy also **gets in the way of partners outside Government – in the voluntary sector and business** – making the contribution that they potentially could. The PAT was told by both sectors that they were unable to contribute as they would like because of lack of information on priorities, what works, sources of, or opportunities for, funding and clear communication by Government of what it wants to achieve.

5.14 The lack of business involvement is particularly problematic. As the analysis in **Chapter 1** notes, young people now face a markedly different jobs market from their predecessors. One of the ways in which young people, particularly those living in areas of high unemployment, can make contact with the world of work is through community involvement by the private sector. This can be through mentoring, work experience or school-business partnerships, or through secondments from business directly into community projects. Whatever form the involvement takes, it is likely to raise the aspirations of the young people involved, and its absence through the lack of focus and strategy outlined above is another opportunity missed.

5.15 The lack of a big picture means that society **all too often fails to recognise the potential that young people themselves have to contribute, in the present and the future**. The focus of much policy making is on individual problems. This tends to brand young people in general as 'a problem' and gets in the way of harnessing their considerable energies to positive ends.

> *"... resources are often misdirected because services are not good enough at listening to what their (sometimes awkward) customers want, as opposed to what the 'experts' doing the strategic planning think they want or should have."*
>
> Big Issue in the North

5.16 Finally, **prevention does not stand much chance with responsibility so fragmented**. So it comes about that despite largely common risk factors for drug taking, teenage pregnancy, offending, school failure, youth homelessness and unemployment, broad-based prevention is left to the voluntary sector, such as many of those projects and initiatives highlighted in **Annex I**. In Government, no-one owns the subject, research and projects are expensive, and the costs and benefits are unlikely to fall in the same place.

How other European countries bring together youth issues

5.17 **Annex G** describes mechanisms in other European countries for making sure young people's needs are properly factored into the design and delivery of services that they need. As **Table 3** shows, the UK is one of the few European countries not to have either a clear Ministerial lead, a Parliamentary Committee or an explicit cross-Government policy.

Table 3: Youth policy organisation in EU countries[107]

Country	Minister for Youth[108]	Ministry for Youth[109]	Parliamentary Committee[110]	Cross-Government youth policy[111]
Austria	●	●		●
Belgium	●[112]	●		●
Denmark				
Finland	●	●	[113]	●
France	●	●		●
Germany	●	●	●	●
Greece		●		
Ireland	●	●		●
Italy	●	●		[114]
Luxembourg	●	●	●	●
Netherlands		●	●	
Portugal	●	●	●	●
Spain	●		●	●
Sweden	●	●	●	●
UK				

Part III – Thinking ahead

Chapter 6: The cost of doing nothing

6.1 The PAT believes that problems described in **Chapters 1** and **2** need to be tackled for two reasons:

- their hugely damaging **social consequences**, for individuals, their families and communities; and
- their **economic consequences** and the waste of resources with which they are associated.

6.2 In each case there is both an immediate set of consequences and longer-term implications.

Social consequences

6.3 The immediate consequences are serious for:

- **young people themselves**, who will not be able to achieve their full potential;
- **their families**, for example where a young person gets into serious trouble at school or with the law, misuses drugs or alcohol or becomes pregnant; and
- **the communities they live in**. A worrying feature of many poor neighbourhoods is the extent to which young people are seen as 'a problem'. In some areas this clearly has its roots in genuinely high levels of anti-social behaviour by children and teenagers. Evidence presented to PAT 8 (*Anti-Social Behaviour*) showed that anti-social behaviour can cause significant physical damage and human misery. In other areas a loss of confidence in young people may be without real justification and can act against community cohesion.

6.4 Young people who suffer from the problems illustrated in **Chapter 2** are likely to continue to feel the effects well into later life. Some of the evidence is summarised in the box opposite.

6.5 More difficult to measure, but equally important, is **the waste of potential**. People who could make a success of their lives in the workplace, family and community instead end up long-term jobless, and raising families in poverty.

Long-term consequences of disengagement

The SEU's *Bridging the Gap*[115] report showed that being out of education, training and employment for six months or more between 16 and 18 is the single most powerful predictor of later unemployment, and is also associated with high levels of depression and poor health, as well as with teenage parenthood (for women), and a criminal record serious enough to be a barrier to employment (for boys).

The SEU's *Teenage Pregnancy*[116] report summarised the evidence that teenage births not only had worse than average outcomes for the child but also led to higher odds of poverty, lack of qualifications, long-term benefit receipt, not being an owner-occupier and experiencing relationship breakdown.

Analysis of the *National Child Development Survey* shows that a young person who experiences a year's unemployment between the ages of 16 and 23 will on average spend 23 per cent of their next ten years unemployed.[117]

The SEU's *Truancy and School Exclusion*[118] report showed the links between truancy and exclusion and educational underachievement, later unemployment and homelessness, as well as the striking links between exclusion and truancy and crime.

DH's *Me, Survive, Out There?*[119] showed how the life chances of care leavers are unacceptably restricted, with those young people leaving care being disproportionately more likely to end up unemployed, homeless and without qualifications.

Economic costs

6.6 There is not enough information to produce a single 'costing' of these problems: there would be huge problems of definition, and the comparability of short- and long-term, total and marginal costs, and costs to the taxpayer and society.

6.7 It is, however, possible to identify costs attached to certain adverse outcomes. **Table 4** identifies some costs that can be tentatively quantified for:

- young people with conduct disorders;
- young people excluded from school;
- young people involved in drug misuse; and
- young people not participating in education, employment or training for six months or more between the ages of 16 and 18.

6.8 Explanation of how these costs were arrived at can be found in the notes in **Annex H**. The costs themselves are divided into the following categories:

- costs to services, arising due to the need to make alternative or emergency provision to deal with problems;
- costs to the wider community, such as benefit expenditure or losses from crime as well as tax and National Insurance contributions forgone; and
- opportunity costs to the individual, such a loss of potential earnings.

6.9 Even here, however, a range of caveats applies:

- some young people will experience more than one of these problems (see **Chapter 1**), so there will clearly be overlaps between different groups, with resultant 'double-counting' of costs. It is therefore important to avoid the temptation to simply add up these costs in an attempt to arrive at some notional headline figure;
- while associations between different problems are recognised, little is known about cause and effect. So, for example, it cannot be said with certainty that a reduction in the number of school exclusions would result in a reduction in the extent of youth offending; and
- the figures just relate to the costs that are *known*. Research in this area is in its infancy, and there will clearly be additional costs that have not yet been explored and quantified.

Table 4: Predicted costs for problems amongst young people

NB. The notes for this table can be found at **Annex H**.

Problem	Services	Community	Opportunity
Conduct disorder (at least four per cent or approximately 20,000 of each year cohort [1])	Alternative educational provision: *c* £219m Additional health provision: *c* £39m Residential care: *c* £60m	Benefits: *c* £22m Offending: *c* £874m	
Excluded from school (approximately 12,300 are permanently excluded from school each year [2])	Alternative educational provision: *c* £22m [3] Offending: *c* £384m [4]	Offending: *c* £167m [5]	
Heroin misuse (no more than one per cent of the population use heroin [6], equating to around 5,000 per age cohort 16–24)		Illegally earned income: *c* £67.5m pa [7]	
Non-participation (approximately 107,000 do not participate for six months or more between 16 and 18 [8])		Potential unemployment benefit: *c* £228m pa [9] Potential lost contributions: *c* £264m pa [10] Potential benefits due to teenage motherhood: *c* £116m pa [11]	Forgone earnings: *c* £763m pa [12]

Chapter 7: What can be done?

7.1 The preceding chapters set out a depressing picture, both in terms of:

- the scale and complexity of problems faced by some young people; and
- the human and financial costs of our failure to tackle this problem more effectively.

7.2 But it would be quite wrong if the PAT were to give the impression that all of the problems this report describes cannot be solved. On the contrary, the PAT has drawn together extensive examples of **good practice** and **underlying principles** that offer a promising way forward on which the PAT has built its recommendations.

Principles underpinning good programmes

7.3 The underlying principles can be put many different ways. But the PAT identified the following seven broad themes common to effective programmes. How these are implemented on the ground is illustrated by reference to the case studies in **Annex I**.

I **The best programmes are thought through from the perspective of young people, including the most marginalised:**

- Involving young people in the design of programmes is almost certainly the best way to ensure that their perspective is accurately reflected. Quality Protects and the proposals put forward by DH on young people leaving care are a good example of such an approach.
- *Fairbridge* and *Youthstart* illustrate some of the key messages that are important in engaging the most marginalised such as:
  - the need to be flexible enough to respond to the needs and priorities of each individual young person;
  - knowing enough about the individual to intervene at the 'right' moment and in the right place – this usually means outreach and the use of detached youth workers who can operate in a young person's territory; and
  - presenting young people with a reasonable 'deal' where a good time is given in return for some application and commitment to more serious issues.
- An element of choice is also important especially in adolescence. Young people are quick to spot where they are being asked to conform to someone else's agenda or are being put through a pre-ordained process and some will 'vote with their feet'. The *Missions Locales* in France, for example (see **Annex G**), only fund projects developed by the young people themselves.
- Using marketing skills. This can affect both the design of programmes, for example, drawing on interests such as IT, music or sport to engage young people; and focusing on positives rather than negatives in how projects are described.

II The best programmes are based on a robust understanding of risk and protective factors. They build on knowledge of why young people tend to get into trouble and what helps to stop them in the first place or rescue them when things have gone wrong:

- This means taking a broad view and understanding the influences, both positive and negative, of family, peer group and community.

- The case studies on *Safe in the City, Communities that Care* and the New York Children's Aid *Pregnancy Prevention Programme* all illustrate particularly well how understanding of risk and protective factors can be used as a basis for action.

III The best programmes are 'joined up', bring together different professions and address all the dimensions that matter to young people's development, including those that are outside Government's traditional scope:

- The case studies for *the Strathmore Centre, Base 51* and *42nd Street* show how different agencies and professions can combine to tackle problems together. They make a powerful case for quality one-stop approaches so young people are not passed from agency to agency, making it harder to build up trusting relationships and easier to slip through the net entirely. An example from the Netherlands – the *Sosjale Joenits* – shows how this has been done elsewhere.

- Equally, the case studies on *Communities that Care*, the *Barnardo's Freagarrach Project* and the *Danish SSP Committees* show how parents and communities can be made part of the solution. Other projects, such as the *Vietnamese Community Association of Western Australia*, harness skills of faith communities to achieve their goals.

IV The best programmes are planned, focused and persistent, with early intervention, intensive action at key transition points, sustained following through, and ways back offered to those who have gone off track:

- Too many interventions fail because they are too late, one-off or withdrawn prematurely. Hence the six-year duration of the New York Children's Aid *Pregnancy Prevention Programme*, and the long-term development programme that underpins the work of the *Fairbridge Project*. Both of these recognise that very disadvantaged young people must be allowed to take things at a realistic pace and though they will often benefit from being removed from their daily environment for a period of time, they need to be provided with appropriate support when they return.

- Projects such as *Communities that Care (UK)* recognise the need for separate stages of audit, design, implementation and aftercare if the changes they set out to achieve are to be deep-seated and long-lasting.

- Focus on key transition points is illustrated by the *Danish SSP* case study which concentrates particularly on transition from primary to secondary school, while the *Oldham Transitions into Work* and *Nottinghamshire Acorn* projects target young people leaving school at 16.

- Programmes supporting young people must be geared to provide support when young people require it and when they show willingness to change previous problematic behaviour. But it should also be accepted that some young people will relapse, and that it might be necessary to extend offers of support, intervention and opportunity to them more than once.

V The best programmes use data and local knowledge to target action and monitor their success:

- This is a key feature of the initial audit that underpins the *Communities that Care* approach and the work of *Leeds City Council.*

VI Some of the best programmes are innovative and proactive, making use of 'non-professional' resources, for example, communities, families and young people themselves:

- While many of the best programmes implement 'what works' principles to achieve their results, others succeed through adopting innovative approaches to particular problems. Others use suitably trained non-professionals to achieve credibility with communities, families and particularly young people, who often do not know what or where help is available and do not trust professionals.

- The *Derby Daytime Potentials, Newcastle Peer Tutoring* and *Bradford Neighbourhood Youth Team* case studies show what can be achieved by using someone with whom the young person can identify, and who has 'been there and done that'.

VII The best programmes are underpinned by proper planning and training:

- Without adequate planning and training, interventions aimed at addressing the complex array of problems experienced by young people will falter. Problems can include confusion over objectives and responsibilities. In other cases, workers may attempt to deal with problems that require specialist help or simply do not have the skills to listen and talk effectively to young people. (Training is also an important way of allowing workers to acknowledge and overcome professional boundaries.) Both *Fairbridge* and *Communities that Care* provide good examples of recognising and overcoming these pitfalls.

- Better planning is needed at regional, district and neighbourhood level, between agencies and within communities. The best local authorities, in their community leadership role, have demonstrated successful co-ordination of district and neighbourhood activity in partnership with young people, and provided training for local residents. The case study of the *Aberdeen Youth Strategy* exemplifies this approach.

Part IV – Getting there

Earlier parts of this report have shown that:

- too many young people are doing badly – often worse than in the past, and than in other countries. Young people from poor backgrounds and poor neighbourhoods and from ethnic minority backgrounds are particularly at risk;

- the PAT believes there is a powerful argument that the Government must take action to change this;

- a good start has been made in some individual policies and services, but more needs to be done in other areas. Above all, the PAT thinks the Government should create a comprehensive and joined-up approach that caters properly for the diversity of the young population; and

- enough is known about young people, and what works in dealing with them, so the further steps necessary can be readily identified.

The final part of this report sets out the PAT's recommendations[120] on how it believes the Government might build on what has been done already, and move towards a comprehensive set of policies and services without overlaps and gaps, based on evidence and giving priority to prevention. The PAT suggests:

- **a strategy with new objectives and structures** to ensure that the Government designs and delivers its youth policy effectively. This would enable it better to harness the potential of the voluntary sector, business, communities and young people themselves, and to keep up with the rapid pace of change in young people's lives **(Chapter 8)**;

- over time, ensuring **prevention** becomes a higher priority for services wherever possible, in particular through a new programme of family support **(Chapter 9)**;

- specific further steps to improve distribution of resources and **individual services**, notably to improve health services for young people, access to leisure and personal development through community service **(Chapter 10)**; and

- a new approach to **designing and delivering services** based on consulting and involving young people and 'starting from where they are' **(Chapter 11)**.

The 2000 Spending Review provides a natural framework for the Government to consider the PAT's recommendations and decide how they should be taken forward.

Chapter 8: Strategy

8.1 The PAT's recommendations in this chapter are designed to:

- help bring coherence to the Government's approach to children and youth at risk, so as to maximise the potential of individual policies;
- ensure that policy is based on proper evidence about young people, their views, and what interventions are effective;
- enable central and local government to work more effectively together with business, the voluntary sector, communities and young people themselves; and
- ensure that Government policy keeps up with the rapid change in young people's lives.

8.2 This needs to happen in an interlocking way, down from the national and strategic level, through local planning and service delivery, to neighbourhoods and the individual.

The national level

> *"Why is there no Minister for Young People when there is a Minister for Women?"*
>
> Young person at Real Deal launch

8.3 In **Chapter 5** the PAT describes the various co-ordination mechanisms that exist or are being set up which affect policy on children and young people, and the work being overseen to join up policy across departmental boundaries. But the PAT believes these still leave the Government without:

- a clearly articulated strategy for children and youth at risk and a set of objectives, built into the spending arrangements;
- a clear Ministerial lead on co-ordination, presentation, and liaison with stakeholders and young people themselves;
- a single Ministerial group to work on these tasks; and
- more than ad hoc machinery to support Ministers and individual departments.

8.4 The PAT's recommendations in this chapter suggest how these gaps might be filled with:

- a set of **objectives** which might form the basis of work in the Spending Review;
- a Youth Affairs Committee and a Youth Unit; and
- improvements to local co-ordination.

RECOMMENDATION 1

The Government should set overarching youth inclusion objectives for its policies and ensure that they are reflected in departmental policies. The objectives might include:

- the Government's aim of ending child poverty in 20 years, and halving it in ten;
- supporting parents and young people in making a success of family life, and providing decent alternatives for those who cannot live in a family structure, until they no longer require care and support;
- helping young people acquire the skills they need for independence, work, citizenship and parenthood, through learning inside and outside school, access to leisure and volunteering opportunities, and support and advice when it is needed;
- supporting young people in vulnerable groups at vulnerable times, paying particular attention to those in poverty and disadvantage, or those who face discrimination because of ethnic origin, disability or gender;
- putting young people at the centre of policies that affect them, organising services round the needs of young people; and
- using what we know to prevent problems if possible, to offer each young person meaningful opportunities to establish themselves in adult life, and not to write young people off.

RECOMMENDATION 2

Ministers should consult on whether the objectives outlined in Recommendation 1 are the right youth inclusion objectives.

RECOMMENDATION 3

The cross-cutting Spending Review on youth at risk, linking with departmental Spending Reviews, should consider how to reflect the overall objectives more closely in departmental programmes. This should include specific Public Service Agreement (PSA) targets for departments, some of which should be cross-cutting.

RECOMMENDATION 4

On conclusion of the Spending Review, the Government should publish a strategy document setting out what has been done and what is still planned.

8.5 These objectives may sound ambitious. But they are no less than young people have the right to expect. The Government is well on the way to putting several key pieces of the jigsaw in place through, for example, its policies on education standards, the Connexions Service and other elements of its new approach to 13–19 education, and new approaches to youth justice and looked after young people.

8.6 Clearly 'Machinery of Government' changes are decisions for the Prime Minister, but the PAT suggests:

- the setting up of a Ministerial Group bringing together all the departments which need to contribute to the strategy and its presentation; and
- clear arrangements for Ministerial leading roles. The central importance of education in policy for young people means DfEE must play an important part in this.

> *RECOMMENDATION 5*
>
> To carry forward the strategy, **the Prime Minister should consider establishing a standing cross-departmental committee or group on children's and youth affairs and giving specific Ministers a leading role.** DfEE must play an important part in this.

> *RECOMMENDATION 6*
>
> **The responsibilities of the Youth Ministers and the Youth Committee might include championing the implementation and further development of a cross-Government strategy** and the underpinning cross-cutting PSAs and speaking/listening on behalf of the Government on youth issues that cut across departmental boundaries, and on the big picture.

8.7 Ministerial machinery of this kind requires cross-cutting official support. The PAT felt this should come from a new Youth Unit or other similar arrangement with the same effect, performing the task as set out in Recommendation 7. The PAT saw strengths in various different options for the departmental location of these tasks. These options include:

- DfEE, as the department responsible for education and the transition to employment;
- the Home Office, building on its existing family policy responsibilities;
- the Department of Health, building on its responsibility for Children's Planning; and
- the Cabinet Office, recognising the need for policy on young people not to be over-identified with any one department.

8.8 Wherever such a Unit were located, it would need to work and draw its members from across Government, and from those with direct experience of work with young people. Its relationship with other cross-cutting work, including the Connexions Service Unit, the Youth Justice Board, the Teenage Pregnancy Unit and Quality Protects and the work of DH on looked after children, would need to be carefully defined.

RECOMMENDATION 7

The Government should establish a Youth Unit or other arrangement with the same effect to support Ministers in carrying forward the strategy, and as a common resource for departments. This should bring together staff from different departments and outside Whitehall. Its broad functions should include:

- driving forward implementation of cross-Government objectives;
- assembling knowledge on: young people; policies and services for them; good practice; risk and prevention; the implications of gender, ethnic origin and disability; and likely future trends;
- supporting Ministers in ongoing refinement of the strategy, including: simplifying the number of initiatives and plans; removing overlaps, gaps and conflicts; and encouraging effective approaches to be mainstreamed rapidly;
- working to remove barriers to effective working, e.g. barriers to information sharing;
- supporting Ministers on presentation of the strategy; and
- drawing together an annual report on the Government's strategy for youth inclusion with the Government making time for this to be debated in Parliament.

(See also Recommendations 10 and 23 for other possible responsibilities of the Youth Unit (or alternative).)

Local service planning and delivery

8.9 As at national level, the PAT believes that the planning and delivery at local level requires a stronger focus. Though new structures have been put in place on a number of specific fronts, there is strong demand from people who work at local level for:

- moving towards a single structure for managing and delivering all services for children and youth at risk, as opposed to several overlapping structures; and
- better information about young people in the area and the services which are available to them.

8.10 A new structure would need to subsume and build on recent developments such as Children's Services Planning, the establishment of YOTs and the commitment to establish the Connexions Service. Proper links between local structures for youth co-ordination and the work of the other PATs, for example, neighbourhood management, as well as local authority neighbourhood renewal co-ordination, will be necessary.

8.11 The PAT's 'job description' for a local co-ordination mechanism is set out in Recommendations 8 and 9 below:

RECOMMENDATION 8

The Government should make clear that it wishes to see effective co-ordination of information about and policies for young people at local level. It should consider the scope for building on the Connexions Service, Children's Services Plans, and other initiatives such as Best Value and the National Strategy for Neighbourhood Renewal. Local authorities and others should be given a chance to express their views.

RECOMMENDATION 9

Key roles for local co-ordination are set out below. Many of these need to be shared with or complement the work of the Connexions Service, depending on its emerging delivery structure:

- gathering information and conducting studies about the characteristics and needs of children and young people locally;
- consulting and involving children and young people;
- identifying areas of special need;
- mapping action already under way;
- identifying and working with appropriate professional and non-professional resources;
- promoting a strategy that aligns different services' priorities and plans, and harnesses other resources;
- promoting information sharing;
- promoting use of a common assessment framework for vulnerable young people; and
- promoting joint outcomes, evaluating impact and tackling barriers.

8.12 The relationship between arrangements for delivering such a local co-ordination mechanism, the Connexions Service and other specific services will need to be designed carefully. To be effective, the local management of the Connexions Service will need to be robustly linked into a structure for ensuring specialised services for youth at risk are available, and that they are well co-ordinated with the personal adviser service.

8.13 The National Strategy for Neighbourhood Renewal is likely to put forward new structures for improving the position of poor areas and neighbourhoods, at both neighbourhood and local authority level. If these structures are to be successful, they must take account of the needs of young people. Local co-ordination mechanisms such as those described above will help them do that.

RECOMMENDATION 10

Consideration should be given in the Spending Review to the possible role of the Youth Unit (or alternative) in encouraging local co-ordination. This could be through distribution of a special 'joining up' fund to create incentives and financial headroom for joint working. This funding could be clawed back from, or additional to, mainstream budgets. This should be measured against other options for improving local co-ordination of youth policies. The outcome of the Spending Review should set out what has been decided.

The caseworking level

8.14 **Chapter 3** describes recent developments which seek to provide more co-ordinated caseworking support for specific groups of young people at risk: YOTs; the 'learning mentors' being introduced as part of the Excellence in Cities initiative; and the Quality Protects new support arrangements for young people who are in or have recently left care. The SEU's *Bridging the Gap*[121] report commits the Government to providing personal advisers for all young people through the Connexions Service.[122]

8.15 For most young people, those not at particular risk of disengagement, this will be a hands-off role, someone available for contact if needed. For those facing more serious problems, the role will be far more active, involving intensive coaching and support, and brokering of educational opportunities. Where specialised help is required (for example, health care or drug counselling or treatment), the adviser will guide (and sometimes accompany) the young person to the appropriate professional through robust referral arrangements.

8.16 The PAT welcomes this development strongly, but wishes to underline five aspects, set out in Recommendation 11 below:

RECOMMENDATION 11

In developing the Connexions Service, particular priority should be given to:

- staffing and professional training;
- the ability to take account of gender differences and to work effectively with young people from different backgrounds, including those from ethnic minorities;
- developing a common framework for assessment and planning for individuals;
- the scope for harnessing community organisations as part of the delivery; and
- having an effective division of responsibilities with arrangements for care leavers and young offenders.

Chapter 9: A more preventative approach

9.1 Earlier chapters of this report have shown that the delivery of many current services is focused on dealing with young people in acute crisis, often at very high unit cost, rather than trying to stop these problems happening in the first place. The PAT believes the philosophy which lay behind the Children Act, 1989 has never been put into practice for a combination of reasons:

- the fact that the costs of crisis intervention fall on **different budgets** from those which might fund earlier preventative activity – and that services which might fund preventative activity would not receive any payback from it;
- the way the **priorities** of services for young people are set out in **legislation and policy guidance**, and the consequences this has for the deployment of resources; and
- **professional cultures**.

9.2 Ensuring a more preventative approach will require:

- a better **understanding** of risk and protective factors (and of adolescent development), and effective approaches to prevention;
- more **information sharing**, so that services which know about a young person at risk can encourage the appropriate intervention where that is from another organisation, and at a service planning level organisations can work together more effectively;
- an increased emphasis on prevention in **professional training**, and in **inspection regimes**; and
- new **targets** for services which are in a position to make effective early interventions, and **funding mechanisms** to support them.

9.3 If the proposals on strategy and co-ordination in **Chapter 8** work well, they should help achieve some of a more preventative approach:

- the Youth Unit's new responsibilities (or those of an alternative) should help to create a comprehensive understanding of risk and protective factors, and to ensure this understanding is disseminated to policy-makers, service planners, and professional and inspection bodies;
- better local co-ordination should promote more sharing of information and inter-service co-operation; and
- effective national arrangements for policy co-ordination should ensure cross-cutting issues of prevention are thought about more effectively. In particular, trends must be tackled early enough to prevent them from becoming problems.

9.4 However, action is also needed to change professional cultures and targets and to set aside funding for prevention. The PAT believes the current Spending Review presents an ideal opportunity for looking at the latter and then taking a Government-wide view on how investment in prevention in one area could reduce resource pressures in another.

RECOMMENDATION 12

The Young People At Risk Spending Review should consider the case for developing family support as a mainstream policy:

- as a first step this Review should look at what is already available and what the development priorities are;
- Ministers should have an early discussion of the links with similar ideas being pursued by the Ministerial Group on the Family, and the recommendations for school-based family support services emerging from PAT 11 on 'Schools Plus';[123]
- departmental responsibilities for elements of the strategy should be made clear;
- proposals should be published for consultation in summer 2000; and
- to inform future policy, the Government should make use of and build on the National Family and Parenting Institute's mapping and evaluation of parenting support, set to be completed by December 2000.

RECOMMENDATION 13

The Young People At Risk Spending Review should also look at the case for identifying a single ring-fenced budget to promote cross-cutting preventative approaches for young people in very disadvantaged risk groups. The aim should be to reduce the risk of later social exclusion amongst looked after children, those suffering serious family conflict, those with severe emotional, behavioural or educational problems and those involved in

RECOMMENDATION 14

DfEE, DH and HO should by summer 2000 publish proposals for a process by which the initial and in-service professional training of social workers, teachers, youth workers, the police, probation and prison officers and health professionals **can be overhauled to increase understanding of risk and protective factors, and effective approaches to prevention.**

9.5 It is worth saying more about the idea on family support. The PAT welcomes the variety of initiatives that should bear on preventing young people and their families experiencing crisis in the young person's teenage years, including Sure Start (currently only in a limited number of areas), the establishment of the Connexions Service and pilots of the On Track multiple intervention programme. However, there is a gap in support for families with children between five and 13, where action might prevent later problems. The Connexions Service will also need to be able to draw on support where problems within families are an obstacle to participation in learning for teenagers. The PAT believes that, even if only in the medium term, a service to support families should become part of the mainstream. In the short term, there is a need for work along the lines of Sure Start to set up models of such support in areas where it is most needed and to test how it can most effectively be delivered.

9.6 The principles on which such a service could be based would be:

- to provide appropriate support for families, including fathers and step-families, focusing on key transition points such as the transition from primary to secondary school;
- to prevent problems from worsening, for example working with schools to ensure the causes of early behavioural problems are identified and dealt with instead of becoming acute in the early teens; and
- to meet the varied needs of the local community, by taking account, for example, of the different needs of ethnic minority communities and family types, and harnessing the skills of voluntary and faith groups to achieve this.

9.7 The main features envisaged for the service are set out in the box below:

Main features of a family support strategy

Local authorities to be under a duty to audit family support already available in their area, including whether such support is relevant to all groups within the community.

Services or referral points in places where they are easily accessible, for example, schools, health centres, family centres and in the workplace, with co-location of professionals from different services.

Promoting family/school partnerships.

Encouraging community and leisure activities that support young people's development and develop parenting skills.

Joint training for professionals.

Encouraging or facilitating self-help by parents and young people.

Information and effective marketing of family support, so that families know where to get help and do not feel it is 'not for them' or a mark of failure to seek it.

Chapter 10: Improving services

10.1 **Chapter 3** drew attention to some of the gaps in the services that young people will need if problems are to be prevented and tackled effectively. Issues identified by the PAT from its consultation and research include:

- overall resourcing of services for children in deprived areas;
- access to advice and treatment on many aspects of health, including sexual health and pregnancy, mental health, and misuse of drugs and alcohol;
- crisis housing and linked support;
- longer-term housing;
- benefits;
- a joined-up approach to dealing with offenders' educational needs;
- leisure (including such basic needs as 'a place to hang out'); and
- public transport.

10.2 There are some welcome developments in all of these areas. However, the PAT believes that the current Spending Review provides the Government with an opportunity to consider how effectively resources are deployed to meet young people's needs in these areas, allowing for the role of the private sector, and where necessary to set new targets with appropriate resources.

> ***RECOMMENDATION 15***
>
> **One measure of success for the Spending Review should be whether it produces an appropriate relationship between need and per capita spending on children and young people in deprived areas.** Research should be commissioned to establish outturn.

> ***RECOMMENDATION 16***
>
> Other Spending Review outcomes the PAT would hope to see are:
>
> - identified targets and funding to provide adequate and effective support for the short- and long-term housing needs of young people (DETR to lead with DH, Department of Social Security (DSS) and the Connexions Service Unit);
> - adequate specialist therapeutic social care and health services especially for drugs, alcohol, mental health and sexual health for young people and their parents, to back up the operation of the Connexions Service;
> - a strategy and targets for improved access to leisure facilities for young people in deprived neighbourhoods; and
> - new targets and funding to bring about a step change in the educational achievement of offenders on the basis of the Government's commitments in the *Bridging the Gap* report.

10.3 Some of the issues are set out in more detail below.

Crisis housing and linked support

10.4 Research evidence supports the proposition that there should be more widely available short-term accommodation:[124]

- to provide respite for parents and young people where tensions have built up or where young people have very high support needs;
- where a young person has left home suddenly and prematurely, to provide a safe place to live in the short term while the next step is sorted out – whether a return to the family home following successful mediation or a move to more permanent accommodation;
- funding pilot schemes and test new models of provision, for example 'crashpad schemes' where local people, appropriately vetted, supported and supervised by social services, make a room and support available on a very short-term basis; and
- young adult short-term fostering and supported lodgings, and professionally managed respite facilities for young people with higher support needs.

Longer-term housing

10.5 *Bridging the Gap*[125] drew attention to lack of housing as a barrier to young people's participation in learning. It recognised the value of services that cover housing and education and training side by side. Such providers should play a part in local delivery of the Connexions Service, and the Service should develop the links it needs with landlords and housing advice agencies. However, as a counterpart to this, and the recommendation above on short-term housing, there should be a review of approaches to the longer-term housing of young people living independently.

Benefits

10.6 *Bridging the Gap* and **Chapter 3** both show that the current system of financial support for young people, particularly under-18s, is fragmented and sometimes fails to support young people in the right way. To deal with this, the Government is piloting Education Maintenance Allowances (EMAs), including the further pilots announced in the SEU's *Teenage Pregnancy*[126] and *Bridging the Gap* reports, and has made a commitment to explore options for a more unified system of financial support in the light of the EMA pilots.

10.7 The PAT believes the initiatives above need to be complemented by actions to ensure that young people get access to the financial support to which they may be entitled under current legislation. Further work is needed to explore if and how the system might be improved. This work should build on that already undertaken by DSS, and on its current processes of continual review. An expert meeting convened by the PAT looked at the delivery of benefits to young people at risk. This meeting produced the detailed proposals set out at **Annex J**. In summary, these suggest that changes might be needed:

- to regulations, to bring the operation of the system more obviously in line with current policy;
- to the provision of information to young people and their advisers;

- to evidence requirements; and
- to staff training and deployment.

10.8 Lessons learned from this work should also be fed into thinking about more unified approaches to financial support, to ensure they cater well for the most vulnerable young people.

10.9 The PAT believes 16 and 17 year olds require special treatment compared with older claimants. The young people for whom JSA Severe Hardship Payments are designed are particularly vulnerable. And the PAT would argue that current policy is already based on the premise that they are different from other claimants – for example, that they can normally be expected to live at home with their parents so rates of benefit for them are lower. Recommendation 18 below suggests how existing research[127] might be built on.

RECOMMENDATION 17

DSS and DfEE should, as a matter of urgency, consider the approach to giving information to young people and their advisers, evidence requirements, staff training and deployment, as these relate to the administration of JSA Severe Hardship Payments and Income Support for young people still in education but estranged from their parents. Detailed proposals for consideration are attached at **Annex J.**

RECOMMENDATION 18

DSS and DfEE should, as a contribution to longer-term thinking on financial support for young people, commission research on how effectively the administration of JSA Severe Hardship Payments and Income Support is meeting the needs of vulnerable 16–17 year olds. If research timescales allow, this should also be done so as to inform policy and administration practice in the short term. Consideration should include: the extent of young people's knowledge of the system; their treatment by Careers Service, Employment Service and Benefits Agency staff; the accuracy of decisions on the award of benefit; and the particular obstacles facing black and other ethnic minority young people.

Improving offenders' educational achievement

10.10 Many young offenders did badly in school.[128] Reoffenders often cannot get a job because of poor education in addition to their criminal record. Yet, as *Bridging the Gap* demonstrated, the criminal justice system, and in particular custodial institutions, have tended to attach a low priority to education and training, and the quality of what *is* provided is often poor.

10.11 Recent developments, notably the establishment of YOTs, the new Detention and Training Orders, and the action to which the Government is committed in *Bridging the Gap*, provide a good basis for remedying this. However, the PAT also believes there is scope in the Spending Review to examine how these changes can be built on. The PAT saw promise in ideas to reward individuals' achievement of defined educational targets with reductions in sentence, and their progress in education after release from custody with rewards and recognition. This might include, for example, a reduction in the time before a conviction is spent. Such an approach sits well with the new Detention and Training Orders, to be introduced from April 2000, which will give flexibility in release date. The PAT would **not** support being soft on offending. But for many, overcoming poor educational achievement and earlier life disadvantage is an enormous challenge that requires support and reward. And all will benefit if reoffending is reduced.

Community and leisure facilities

10.12 *Bridging the Gap* committed the Government to developing a Youth Card to provide young people engaged in learning with access to a range of leisure, transport and other discounts. The PAT believes one way of making the card still more attractive would be for the Government to define a package of *entitlements* to leisure and transport for which the card would be a passport. It could, for example, guarantee young people, who had participated in post-16 learning for a minimum period, free driving lessons, holiday discounts, free tickets for arts and sports events etc.

> ***RECOMMENDATION 19***
>
> **Thinking on the leisure and transport aspects of the Youth Card should be bold.** It should consider whether there are specific entitlements that should be built in to reward learning achievement, e.g. free driving lessons, holiday discounts, free tickets for arts and sports events etc.

10.13 Since it started, the National Lottery has provided funds for many projects that benefit young people, including those at risk of exclusion. Last year the Government altered the Policy Directions funding bodies to emphasise support for children and young people.[129] The distribution bodies are currently actively considering a joint scheme for the construction or refurbishment of community facilities in the most deprived neighbourhoods. Even such modest facilities as a place where young people could meet their friends without disturbing other residents could be of significant practical benefit, and could provide a base for outreach activities for health, education and crime prevention activities.

> ***RECOMMENDATION 20***
>
> **The Lottery distribution bodies should, in any joint scheme for community facilities, include improvements in leisure facilities for young people as a priority element.**

Volunteering and community activity

10.14 The PAT welcomes the Millennium Volunteers programme's recognition of the potential of volunteering and community activity to promote individuals' learning and personal development and to benefit their communities, including other young people. It is an ambitious step towards creating a national approach to young citizens' service. A range of other policy developments is also relevant, including:

- citizenship education;
- the summer camps programme announced by the Secretary of State for Education and Employment, following discussion with the Department for Culture, Media and Sport (DCMS), in January this year;
- the proposals for 'graduation' in the SEU's *Bridging the Gap* report;
- the ambitions set out in the Government's policy document on the Connexions Service, published in February 2000, for involving young people in its delivery;[130]

- the plans by HO to increase community involvement and voluntary activity following the report of the PAT on Community Self-help;[131] and
- the plans by DCMS and its sponsored bodies to increase young people's involvement in cultural and sporting activities following the report of the PAT on Arts and Sport.[132]

10.15 One useful task which the new co-ordinating mechanisms proposed in **Chapter 8** could perform is to promote discussion across departments on ways in which the links between these developments and the Millennium Volunteers programme could be strengthened to promote even more vigorously the development of citizenship and community involvement by young people.

RECOMMENDATION 21

Under the auspices of the new co-ordinating machinery for work on young people, DfEE should work with other relevant departments to develop by end-2000 proposals linking together across Government the range of initiatives described above with the Millennium Volunteers programme.

Chapter 11: Designing policy around the needs of young people

11.1 The PAT argued in **Chapter 5** that services provided for young people at risk are frequently designed around the needs of completely different groups of people. Remedying this requires:

- policy makers and service managers to be better briefed about youth at risk;
- decision makers at all levels to be involved in effective two-way communication with young people; and
- flowing from this, a new and 'smarter' approach to designing policies for young people.

11.2 The proposals in **Chapter 8** for better co-ordination nationally and locally will help with the first of these aims.

11.3 For the rest, the PAT does not believe there is a need to start from scratch. A variety of effective mechanisms for consultation and involvement already exist in the voluntary and local government sectors – such as the *Real Deal* and *Birmingham Youth Consultation* initiatives highlighted in **Annex I** – and the recommendations that follow draw on their experience. However, the picture is patchy and, with the exception of recent developments like Quality Protects and the *Listen Up* exercise,[133] central Government has been comparatively uninvolved.

11.4 The PAT believes the key to effective practice in this area is not a uniform 'one-size-fits-all' approach. Organisations need to design their consultation arrangements around the objectives they are trying to achieve, the kind of business they are in, and the young people they need to work with. Issues of gender and different ethnic minority background must also be considered.

RECOMMENDATION 22

All Government departments and agencies whose work has a significant impact on young people should have a policy of consulting and involving them in policy development and service delivery which affects them. The Youth Unit should facilitate this and set out in its annual reports what has been done.

RECOMMENDATION 23

Local authorities, in keeping with Best Value principles, and the voluntary sector should also have policies for consulting and involving young people.

11.5 While recognising that different styles are needed in different settings, the PAT has put forward (set out in the box below) a set of principles for effective consultation:

Consultation and involvement: principles

Consultation:

- should be a process, not a one-off event;
- should involve dialogue, i.e. organisations' response to young people's views needs to be fed back to young people and they in turn have a chance to comment further;
- should ensure consultation and involvement include young people from ethnic minority groups, those with disabilities, and those most disengaged from society. Methods should be sensitive to gender differences, and suitable for the whole range of young people who need to be consulted;
- should be sensitive to young people's expectations about how they want to be treated and how they wish to respond, not based on adult procedures and timescales; and
- should regularly renew the range of young people involved in the process, and adapt the process to what works with new groups.

The key questions are:

- Who is the consultation aimed at and why is it being done?
- For how long is the consultation expected to continue?
- How will feedback and comments be dealt with?

11.6 The PAT believes there is real potential for policy that is better informed by facts and assembled experience, by dialogue with young people, and by the principles of effective working outlined in the previous chapter. Policy could take off in exciting new directions, incorporating young people's enormous potential while tackling the problems which cause so much trouble for them and others.

11.7 It is not only policies focused on young people that need to be made 'smarter'. The PAT has suggested in **Chapter 5** that:

- there is often too little recognition of the needs of young people within general regeneration programmes. The parallel tendency of such programmes to neglect the needs of ethnic minorities has a particular impact on young people who are members of such groups; and
- where funding is provided, it is too often provided on a short-term basis which offers no guarantee of reward for success. Success is not even measured. Emphasis is on innovation and new approaches to the detriment of what has been tried, and works. Some kinds of organisation (notably those serving ethnic minority communities) feel particularly disadvantaged by this approach to funding.

11.8 Better structures for co-ordinating policy and service delivery for young people locally and nationally (**Chapter 8**) should provide a means of ensuring that national programmes, and decisions on how they are deployed locally, take proper account of the needs of young people. However, the PAT believes that the ground-rules for such programmes should be bolstered through specific recognition of the needs and priorities of young people. This is a critical issue in the SEU's consideration of regeneration programmes as part of the National Strategy for Neighbourhood Renewal.

RECOMMENDATION 24

As part of its proposals on the future deployment of regeneration funding within the National Strategy for Neighbourhood Renewal, the Unit should:

- recognise the need for national regeneration programmes to include specific objectives relating to young people, and means for ensuring those objectives are achieved; and
- suggest means by which those deploying programmes locally can be held to account for the effectiveness with which they have achieved outcomes relating to young people.

Annex A: Remit and acknowledgements

Remit:

The report meets PAT 12's remit, set out in the SEU's September 1998 report on deprived neighbourhoods.

An action team led by the SEU will report on:

- the key costs of youth disaffection and the most effective interventions for preventing it;
- the respective roles of the different agencies including schools, the Careers Service, the Youth Service, TECs and FE colleges, police and probation, health and social services, DATs, and the voluntary sector and business;
- how work to reduce youth disaffection can be planned, targeted and co-ordinated more rigorously;
- what can be done to support families with older children and deal with problems such as conflicts with step-parents, children leaving home prematurely; and
- how the design of services can take greater account of the perspectives of young people.

Goal:

- to identify what needs to be done to develop cost-effective preventative work with disaffected young people in poor neighbourhoods; and
- to develop an action plan with targets to take this forward.

Acknowledgements

In addition to its work on this report, the PAT was closely involved in the SEU's *Bridging the Gap* report which focused on 16–18 year olds not in education, employment or training. The PAT's discussions were informed by:

- consultation exercises in 1999 on the 16–18s project and on the PAT's remit, to which there were over 500 responses from a range of interested institutions, organisations and individuals;
- visits to disadvantaged neighbourhoods and to projects working with young people;
- a programme of research looking at existing literature, a cohort study and survey data, as well as a series of interviews with parents of, and those working with, young people in poor neighbourhoods; and
- discussions with groups of 'practitioners', including independent youth workers, local authority youth workers and people working in local drug projects.

As the findings of the PAT emerged, discussions were held with a variety of groups of young people, many of whom came from the neighbourhoods and 'at risk' groups discussed in this report. The reactions of the young people to the PAT's ideas, and subsequent discussion of the sense they made in the light of the young people's own life experiences, proved invaluable in shaping and 'reality checking' the recommendations in this report.

The PAT is particularly grateful to young people from the following:

- Bangladesh Welfare Association, Burnley
- Carnegie Young People's Initiative
- Communities against Poverty, Liverpool
- Darwen Youth Group, Lancashire
- Feltham YOI, London
- Groundwork, Hackney
- Kaleidoscope, London
- Sherborne House, London
- Triumph and Success, Sheffield
- Warren Centre, Hull

Members of the PAT were drawn from a wide range of organisations in all sectors (full list of members at **Annex B**). The SEU is grateful to all members of the PAT, and the numerous people who were not members but whose contributions were invaluable. This report would not have been possible without their generous time and efforts.

The SEU's remit covers England only and references within the report to 'national' initiatives relate to England only (unless otherwise specified). However, the Scottish Executive, Welsh Assembly and the Northern Ireland Office share the analysis underlying the report and the importance given to tackling the issues. The devolved administrations will be considering whether the action set out in the report could be applied in the light of the particular circumstances present in each country.

Annex B: Membership of PAT 12

Champion Minister

Rt Hon Paul Boateng MP	Minister of State, Home Office and Deputy Home Secretary

Members

Moira Wallace	Chair, Social Exclusion Unit
Caroline Abrahams	NCH Action for Children
Victor Adebowale	Centrepoint
Andrew Allberry	Department of the Environment, Transport and the Regions
Sarah Benioff	Crime Concern
Tom Bentley	Demos
Paul Bolt	Department for Culture, Media and Sport
Katharine Bramwell	Home Office
Virginia Burton	Home Office
John Bynner	Institute of Education, University of London
Balbir Chatrik	Unemployment Unit and Youth Aid
Felicity Clarkson	Prison Service
Sue Cockerill	Women's Unit, Cabinet Office
Chris Corrigan	Department of Health
Sue Duncan	Department of Social Security
David Forrester	Department for Education and Employment
Carol Freer	Department of Social Security
John Graham	Social Exclusion Unit
Ravi Gurumurthy	Social Exclusion Unit
Cathy Havell	Centrepoint
Simon Hickson	Home Office
Nicholas Holgate	HM Treasury
Liam Hughes	Bradford Metropolitan District Council
Hilary Jackson	Home Office
Tom Jeffrey	Department of Health
Pat Kneen	Joseph Rowntree Foundation
Jonathan Lane	Home Office
Adrian Leather	Burnley Borough Council
Julie O'Mahoney	Social Exclusion Unit
Denise Platt	Department of Health
David Reardon	Social Exclusion Unit
Claire Reindorp	Crime Concern
Andrew Shaw	Department of Social Security
Rob Smith	Department for Education and Employment

Ian Sprawson	Department of Social Security
Laurie Taylor	Government Office for London
Mike Trace	Deputy UK Anti-Drugs Co-ordinator
Claire Tyler	Department for Education and Employment
Phil Ward	Northern Foods
Michael Watson	Education Researcher
Martin Wheatley	Social Exclusion Unit
Jeremy Whittle	Windsor Fellow on attachment to Social Exclusion Unit
Howard Williamson	Cardiff University

Secretariat

Phil Clapp	Social Exclusion Unit
Judith Simpson	Social Exclusion Unit
Sandra Walkey	Social Exclusion Unit

Annex C: Young people from ethnic minority communities in poor neighbourhoods[134]

This Annex brings together the PAT's analysis of the problems faced by young people from ethnic minority groups.

1 The PAT's remit, in common with those of other PATs, required it to look specifically at the position of young people from ethnic minority groups. The main report recognises the significance of the obstacles many young people from such groups face in their teenage years, and the particular impact on them of the current handling of the 'big picture' and of individual services. It tries to take account of their specific needs and circumstances in what it says about effective practice, and in its recommendations.

2 The purpose of this annex is to bring together in one place the PAT's analysis of the position of young people from ethnic minority groups, which is inevitably fragmented by the structure of the main report. Its three sections examine:

- some important points on location, demography and family structure;
- the specific additional ways in which young people from ethnic minority groups are often disadvantaged; and
- the ways in which the PAT's conclusions and recommendations should contribute to an improvement in outcomes for them.

Location, demography and family structure

3 There are no figures showing the exact extent to which young people from ethnic minorities are concentrated in the most disadvantaged areas. However, the following facts seem fairly conclusive:

- over two-thirds of people from ethnic minority groups live in four large metropolitan areas, London, the West Midlands, Greater Manchester and West Yorkshire, which between them account for less than a quarter of the white population – and contain many of the most deprived areas and neighbourhoods;[135]
- over half the ethnic minority population is concentrated in just 29 local authorities (22 of them in London boroughs), accounting for just 11 per cent of the white population;[136] and
- the 44 areas highlighted in the Unit's 1998 report on neighbourhood renewal[137] contain proportionately four times as many people from ethnic minority groups as other areas:
  - these concentrations are significant, but they should not lead to neglect of small populations, either in predominantly white areas, or small communities of a particular origin in more diverse areas; and

– the ethnic minority population is disproportionately young: 48 per cent of the ethnic minority population is under 24 years of age, compared to 31 per cent of the white population. Forty per cent of the Bangladeshi and Pakistani population is under 16 – compared with only 20 per cent of the white population.[138]

4 There are also some important points about family structure:

- only seven per cent of Pakistani/Bangladeshi households are single person (compared with 28 per cent of white households);[139]
- by the age of 24, young people from white and south Asian groups are twice as likely to be married as African-Caribbean people of the same age;[140]
- less than a third of African-Caribbean children are being brought up in a household with two parents;[141] and
- a disproportionate number (20 per cent) of looked after children are from ethnic minority backgrounds.[142]

How young people from ethnic minority groups experience additional disadvantage

5 The PAT tried to assemble information about young people from ethnic minority groups not just in terms of how their position is better or worse than white young people, but whether or not the disparities are getting better or worse.

6 From the information assembled it is clear that:

- not all groups are equally disadvantaged compared to white young people; however,
- most groups are worse off than white young people in many important aspects of their lives; and
- the trend is towards a greater disparity in a disturbing number of cases.

7 The rest of this annex provides a brief commentary on the main issues.

Income

8 **Figure 4** below shows the extent to which households from different ethnic minority groups are poor.[143]

Figure 4: Percentage of households below half average income, by ethnic group

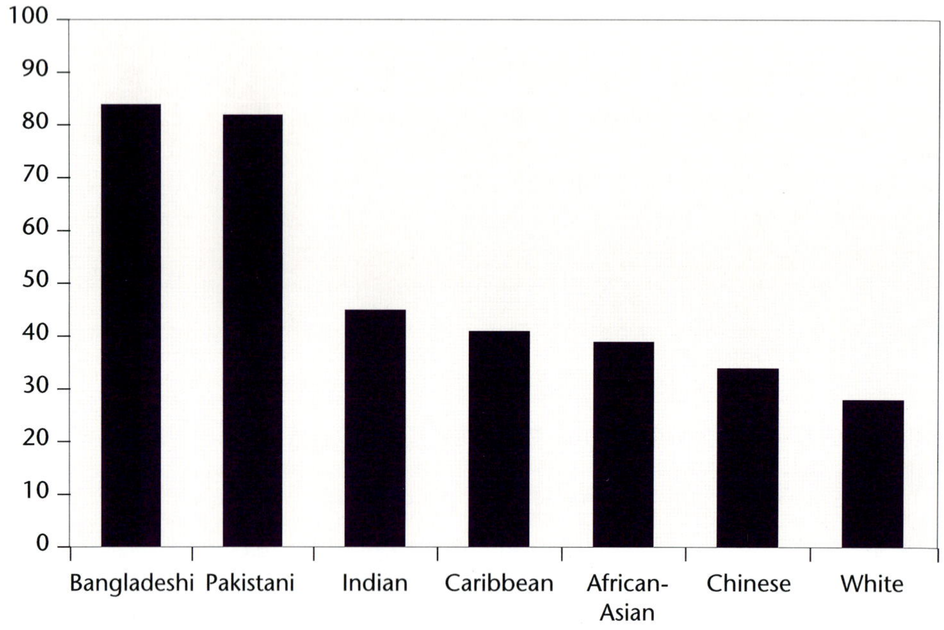

9 Certain types of family, housing tenure and qualification levels are strongly related to persistently low income. Proportionately more households from ethnic minority groups are in some of these categories, notably couples and single people with children, and those headed by workless adults of working age, those with no qualifications and those renting social housing.[144]

Health

10 While there is some information on the general health of ethnic minority communities, there is relatively little specifically on young people from these communities. However, there is evidence that (at age 11) those who were migrants had better health than non-migrants (those born in the UK), that is, that ethnic variations in health could be the result of the negative impact of the UK environment. There is other evidence that for ethnic minority people of all ages poor health is related to the length of time people have been in Britain.

11 Infant mortality rates are around 100 per cent higher for children of mothers born in the Caribbean or Pakistan.[145]

12 Several ethnic minority groups the SEU consulted for its *Teenage Pregnancy* report[146] expressed the view that sexual health services were frequently not designed in a way that would reach specific groupings, and this was especially so for young people.[147]

Homelessness/housing

13 Nearly half of the young people using Centrepoint's temporary housing services are black and there are more young black women than men at the project. Black women currently make up 43 per cent of Centrepoint's female population.[148]

14 While there has been some improvement in the housing of ethnic minorities since the early 1980s:

- they are still more likely to be less satisfied than their white counterparts with their homes, and to live in poorer quality and less popular types of accommodation, regardless of tenure;[149]
- African-Caribbean and Bangladeshi groups are disproportionately concentrated in social housing;[150]
- Bangladeshi and Pakistani households disproportionately suffer from overcrowding;[151]
- Bangladeshi and African-Caribbean flat dwellers are over-represented in medium to high rise accommodation;[152] and
- Pakistani and Bangladeshi owners tend to be concentrated in poor condition terraced housing.[153]

Education

15 The proportion of ethnic minority pupils gaining five or more GCSEs at grades A*–C has increased since 1994. However, there are some striking variations:

- across England as a whole, 47 per cent of white pupils achieve this standard compared with 33 per cent of Bangladeshi pupils and 29 per cent of both Pakistani and African-Caribbean pupils;[154]
- in Birmingham (which has the largest *number* of ethnic minority pupils in the country), although the overall proportion of pupils reaching this standard increased, the gap between African-Caribbean pupils (the lowest achieving group) and white pupils (the highest achieving group) grew by three percentage points. Just over one in three white pupils achieved at least five higher grades, but only one in seven African-Caribbean pupils scored as well;[155]
- in Brent (the LEA with the highest *proportion* of ethnic minority pupils in the country) there was an increase of 1.5 per cent in the gap between south Asian and African-Caribbean pupils;[156]
- in Tower Hamlets, which is home to almost a quarter of all Bangladeshi children between five and 15 years old in this country, 30 per cent of Bangladeshi girls and 25 per cent of boys achieved five GCSEs at grades A*–C in comparison with 21 per cent and 18 per cent of white girls and boys respectively.[157]

16 Since 1994, permanent exclusions have risen by some 13 per cent and across all ethnic groups. Within this though, African-Caribbean pupils have been shown to be five times more likely to be excluded than white. Pupils of mixed race are also disproportionately likely to be excluded.[158]

17 In 1996–97, of those in higher education, 13 per cent were from ethnic minority groups, a little over double their representation in the population as a whole. In enrolment for further education courses, African-Caribbean and white young people were more likely to be studying on vocational courses, and young Asian people more likely to enrol on academic courses.[159]

18 The SEU's *Bridging the Gap* report on 16–18 year olds not in education, work and training shows the additional disadvantage experienced in post-16 education and training by young people from ethnic minority groups, and the links between such disadvantage and earlier educational experience and achievement.[160]

Employment

19 Thirty-three per cent of Indian/African-Asian young people aged 16–19 are unemployed, and over 50 per cent of African-Caribbean, Pakistani and Bangladeshi young people of the same age.[161] Two-fifths of 16 year olds from ethnic minorities not in full-time education were out of work in 1997, compared to one-fifth of their white counterparts.[162] This does not improve with age: 13 per cent of men aged under 35 from ethnic minority backgrounds have spent more than a third of their lives since the age of 16 in unemployment, compared with just seven per cent of young white men.[163]

20 Even the possession of qualifications is no guarantee of employment. For those with degree or higher level qualifications, the unemployment breakdown by ethnic origin for all ages shows 11 per cent of African-Caribbean and six per cent of south Asian people were unemployed compared to three per cent of white people. For those with qualifications equivalent to A-level, 17 per cent of African-Caribbean and 14 per cent of south Asian people were unemployed compared to five per cent of white people.[164]

21 A Commission for Racial Equality 'testing exercise' in 1996 supplied equally qualified job candidates of different racial backgrounds. It confirmed that the south Asian candidates found it three times as hard, and the African-Caribbean candidates five times as hard, to get an interview compared to white candidates.

Crime

22 There is plenty of evidence that people from ethnic minorities suffer disproportionately from the consequences of crime, but little on young people specifically. However, data from the British Crime Survey suggests young people under 24 are responsible for over half of the racially motivated incidents (this data includes crimes not reported to the police).[165]

23 Young people from ethnic minorities are likely to be particularly affected by the extent to which people from ethnic minority communities are stopped and searched or arrested. Of a million people stopped and searched in 1998–99, nine per cent were black, five per cent were Asian and one per cent were classified as 'other non-white'. Black people were six times more likely to be stopped and searched than white people. Of the just over 190,000 people cautioned in 1998–99, six per cent were black, four per cent were Asian and one per cent were classified as 'other non-white'.[166]

24 Among offenders, sentences for ethnic minority offenders tend to be longer, and African-Caribbean young men are disproportionately likely to be in custody.[167]

25 The 1996 British Crime Survey showed that ethnic minority 16–29 year olds were much *less* likely to have used drugs than their white counterparts: 46 per cent of white young people said they had taken drugs, compared with 31 per cent of African-Caribbean, 22 per cent of Indian and 16 per cent of Pakistani and Bangladeshi young people.[168]

Conclusions and recommendations

26 It is wrong to generalise about the position of young people from ethnic minority groups. There are important differences between, and within, particular groups in the nature and scale of disadvantage. However, the analysis above supports, in the PAT's view, a conclusion that they are disproportionately disadvantaged. Some, whose experience of discrimination, poverty and other forms of exclusion is particularly acute, pose formidable challenges for policy and re-engagement work.

27 The PAT suggests that this conclusion needs to be reflected in the development of the new approach to youth at risk which it sets out in the main report in a number of ways:

- **at national level**, the objectives need to be based on proper evidence about young people from ethnic minority groups. Information needs to be detailed enough to pick up the distinctions between and within groups, and between young men and young women. One of the main functions of the proposed new co-ordinating mechanism should be to ensure that Government develops a proper evidence base that is used effectively to inform both cross-cutting policy development and individual departmental programmes;

- **at local level**, the new mechanisms proposed need to build up an information base about the ethnic minority groups in the local youth population, to establish where current services do not meet their needs effectively, and to ensure that steps are taken to meet those needs. People from local ethnic minority communities (for example, voluntary sector, faith and business leaders) should be included in the new structures;

- **at the caseworking level**, the diversity of the local community needs to be reflected, either in the recruitment into mainstream services of staff who know how to work with particular communities, or in the franchising of services to appropriate voluntary and community organisations;

- people with knowledge of the circumstances of and effective practice in working with ethnic minority communities should be involved in the development of new approaches to **prevention and family support**. Further policy development in this area should ensure it is designed to reflect the diversity of disadvantaged young people and their families both in its analysis of risk factors and in the way new approaches are developed;

- work on policy development on the recommendations for **individual services** should be carried out on the same principles; and

- one of the main reasons for systematically building **consultation and involvement with young people** into the way policies and services are delivered is to ensure that the aspirations and needs of ethnic minority groups are understood and acted on. Consultation and involvement must therefore be designed to include them. They should balance the need to bring young people from different backgrounds together with consultation with specific groups, particularly those with limited English or whose culture discourages public involvement.

Annex D: Support for families

> *"Well, once you get your kids you love them, but when they become teenagers you hate them as well. They are so belligerent and rude. I can remember years ago I heard a teenager answer her mother back and I said my kids would never be like that, but they are just the same... they've got this awful attitude, arrogant and rude and think they know it all. I can't believe I was ever like that."*
>
> Lone mother and widow, Bradford[169]

This annex looks at the needs of young people in the context of their families, and at the needs of parents in supporting their children – especially teenage children.

Why do families need support?

Families are changing

1 Families and family life have changed dramatically in the last 20 to 30 years. The box below illustrates some of the trends:

- Four in every ten children are now born outside marriage.[170]
- Two out of three young people cohabit before they marry, compared with one in eight 20 years ago.[171]
- More than four in ten marriages are now likely to end in divorce;[172] since 1971, the proportion of marriages which are remarriages has more than doubled from 17 per cent to 40 per cent.[173]
- Lone parenthood has trebled in the last 20 years from just over half a million in the early 1970s to 1.7 million today;[174] the proportion of lone parents who are single, never-married mothers has more than doubled in the last 20 years from 17 per cent to 38 per cent.[175]
- The proportion of married and employed mothers with pre-school age children has doubled over the last 20 years from a quarter to a half.[176]
- The number of conceptions to girls under 16 has increased by ten per cent since 1993.[177]

Young people's lives have changed too

2 Over the same period, the lives of young people themselves have also changed considerably, as the box below shows:

- By the time they reach 16, more than one in four children will have experienced the divorce of their parents.[178]
- One in five children live in lone parent families – three times the proportion in 1971 – and one in 12 live in step-parent families.[179]
- Over three-quarters of children living in lone parent families experience poverty, compared with less than a fifth of those living in two parent families.[180]
- Nearly one in three children live in poor households (those with an annual net income below half the national average) compared with one in ten 20 years ago.[181]
- Between 1977–78 and 1997–98, both the proportion of no-earner households[182] and the proportion of children in workless households more than doubled.[183]

Why do these changes matter?

3 Families are where children and young people should receive care, support, love and stability. For many, they are the first port of call for advice, guidance and assistance. Some are able to offer financial assistance, others simply access to a wider network of social support.

4 Families are where young people should develop emotional maturity. They should provide supervision, discipline and role models, and a secure place from which to explore adulthood and prepare for independence.

5 During the teenage years tensions between parents and their children are often at their greatest. Yet it is during these years that young people have to make important decisions about their future. The pressures young people experience – from peers, from school, from the media – all combine to make this a period of great uncertainty.

6 While most parents and young people are able to cope with these pressures, an increasing number find family life is characterised by instability, poverty and conflict. Research shows how these factors – individually or in combination – can damage the life chances of young people:

- children of separated parents are more likely to have behavioural problems, to suffer from ill-health, to be taken into care, to use drugs, to offend and to die younger;[184]
- teenage parents are more likely to experience poor health, poverty and relationship breakdown;[185] and
- the increase in youth homelessness during the 1980s and early 1990s (and in particular the rise in the number of homeless 16–17 year olds) is in part due to the increase in the number of remarriages and a lack of parental support.[186]

But do these changes matter more in poor neighbourhoods?

> *"You live below the poverty line and children need this and they need that... the financial pressures are crippling, especially when their father has retracted everything. If someone gave me money, my mum or someone, then it will go straight on the children, on things they need, on a trip or something, I can never think about myself."*
>
> Lone parent, Bradford

7 **Chapter 1** showed how problems such as poor health, unemployment, poverty and victimisation are more prevalent in deprived neighbourhoods. All can seriously exacerbate family conflict, and make parents feel inadequate and incapable of building and sustaining healthy and effective family relationships.

8 Children living in certain families are particularly vulnerable. For example, those living in lone parent families are more likely to live in workless and/or poor households. Nearly three million children live in lone parent households and a similar number in workless households. Two-thirds of the former and four-fifths of the latter are poor. Research published recently has also shown that children and young people from reconstituted families are particularly at risk of becoming runaways.[187]

9 Children living with just one parent are nearly three times as likely to be poor as those living with two parents. Those living in workless households are nearly seven times more likely to be poor than those living in households with at least one full-time worker.[188]

10 **Figure 5**[189] shows clearly how these vulnerable families – in particular lone parents – are concentrated in the most deprived metropolitan local authorities. Whereas in the ten most deprived districts about one in four of all teenagers live in a lone parent family (and in the most deprived area about one in three), in the ten least deprived it is about one in six.

Figure 5: Variation of family structure with area deprivation

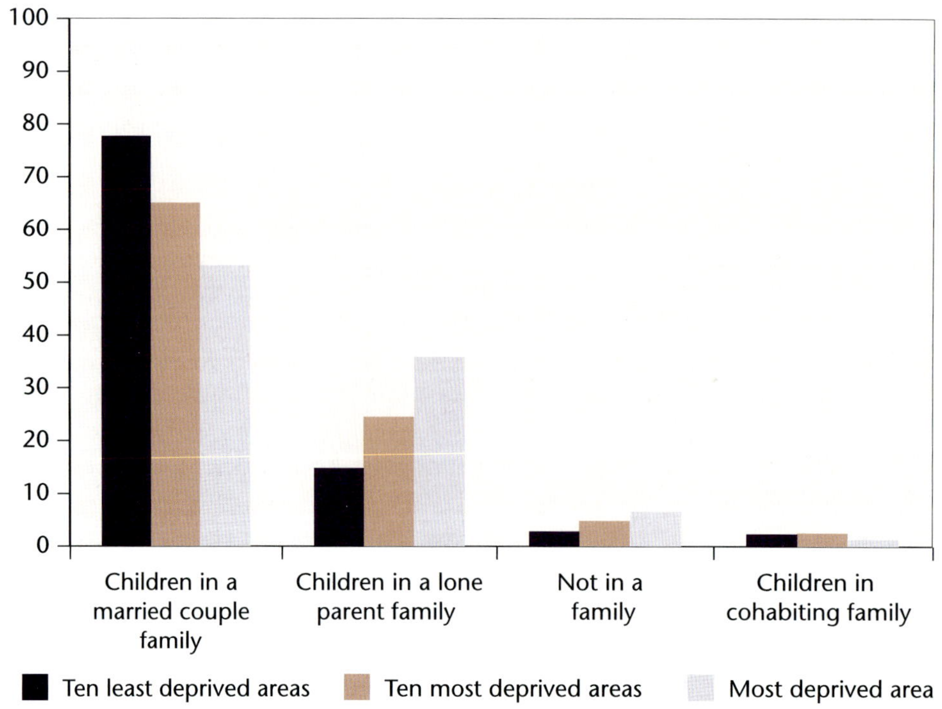

11 Children from ethnic minority backgrounds, also heavily concentrated in deprived areas, are even more likely to live in poverty. Three-quarters of all Pakistani and Bangladeshi children live in poor households (compared with a third of all children).[190]

12 Families caring for children with disabilities also face additional problems. Parents often find it very difficult to mix caring with paid employment[191] and that housing provision is unsuitable for their needs.[192] Evidence suggests that these problems will of course be exacerbated in deprived areas, and where a family has more than one disabled child to support.[193]

13 To summarise, families living in deprived neighbourhoods are likely to face more acute problems, such as long-term unemployment, sickness or disability and divorce or separation. They are less able to offer material support, such as furniture and rent. And where parents have separated or where relationships are fraught, they simply have less **capacity** to meet the needs of their children, material or otherwise.

> *"I'd just like to be able to provide for them better really... It's hard sometimes when some of their mates are coming round, you know – 'Oh look at this' – a brand new top, you know, 50, 60 quid, and you're like that, you've no chance... It's just hard really."*
>
> Unemployed father[194]

Can families prevent social exclusion?

14 Families **can** reduce the risk of social exclusion. A stable and supportive family can protect young people growing up in disadvantaged areas, balancing some of the risks they face and helping them to achieve their potential and make a successful transition to adulthood.

15 **Chapter 1** set out the main risk factors that can influence the lives of young people. These risks can be offset by positive influences in the family that can protect young people from social exclusion. These include:

- a strong relationship with one or both parents or some other member of the family, such as a grandparent;
- a stable relationship between two parents who provide consistent parenting messages;
- continuing and positive contact with the family after leaving home;
- positive role models who set clear, high expectations;
- active involvement in family life; and
- feeling valued or respected by a parent or parents.

16 The SEU's *Bridging the Gap*[195] report also showed that parents can play an important role in persuading children to stay in learning post-16 and support them in doing so. Similarly, the SEU's *Teenage Pregnancy*[196] report showed that parents have a crucial part to play in reducing teenage pregnancy rates by preparing young people far more effectively for sex and relationships, ensuring that they have the means to deal with the pressure to have sex too early in their lives.

What kind of support do parents need?

17 Supporting families is not just about compensating for a shortage of financial or material wealth, but also about promoting healthy relationships. But it must be recognised that the quality of relationships can be affected by material issues that a better-off family might not have to face. Children (and especially teenagers) are all exposed to the same materialist pressures and often want the same things, irrespective of the incomes of their parents.[197]

18 Parents today often feel inadequate, out of their depth, confused about their role and stressed. Some parents are able to cope with little difficulty, but many need and want help and support, as the responses to the HO consultation document *Supporting Families*[198] clearly showed.

19 In a survey of 2,000 parents in poor neighbourhoods,[199] two-thirds stated that they would like more information about parenting and about half said they would like help or support at least sometimes. The most common requests were for advice and support on:

- what to expect in terms of 'normal' behaviour at different ages;
- how to deal with problematic behaviour;
- advice on matters relating to their child's education;
- the pros and cons of different ways of disciplining their children;
- how to parent teenagers;
- how to talk to their children about growing up, their bodies and sex;
- how to deal with sibling rivalry; and
- how children learn.

20 The survey also asked parents to list their preferred sources of advice and support on parenting teenagers. Leaflets and the media were supported by half of the parents consulted, with informal discussion groups and parenting classes among other ideas.

What support is currently available for families?

21 At the national level, the interdepartmental Ministerial Group on the Family, chaired by the Home Secretary, is developing a number of national initiatives to support families, including services for parents of teenagers. These initiatives include:

- publishing *Supporting Families*, the first Government paper setting out a coherent set of strategies for family policy;
- the setting up of the National Family and Parenting Institute, and the funding of it to map the provision of family support available across the country by December 2000;
- exploring ways of communicating with parents, potentially via the Child Benefit database;
- the funding of projects mapping provision of parenting support for teenagers, identifying and developing best practice. This will be funded in 2000–01 to the sum of £780,000;

- working to reduce the negative impact of relationship breakdown and re-partnering on children; and
- a programme of research and dialogue with young men and women on the gender-specific issues affecting them.

22 At the local level, social services departments remain the major funders of family support services. However, resource constraints and a child protection focus have made it difficult for social services to offer a comprehensive service. And because some parents fear social services, the family support services they run may not always reach the most vulnerable children and families. For this reason, social services departments often contract with voluntary sector providers to operate services such as family centres on their behalf.

23 Respondents to the PAT's consultation drew attention to the current lack of support for parents of teenagers and for teenagers themselves. This was felt to be a particular problem for families that are poor or where relationships are fraught.

> *"There are few services for young people affected by family conflict and this is much needed. In one area, over 2,500 per month call a help line provided via the local authority and most calls are about this issue."*
>
> Somerset County Council Youth Service

24 And research shows that the majority of young people themselves also want support, in particular when confronted with parental relationship breakdown and divorce/separation, where they feel they should be formally consulted (as currently occurs in Scotland) or in cases of domestic violence.[200]

25 A few pioneering family support schemes, particularly parenting programmes, are beginning to address the needs of young people and their families. But concerns remain. There is, for example, a particular lack of programmes aimed at supporting parents and adolescents in resolving family conflicts. One review of parenting programmes found that these were least likely to be accessed by ethnic minority parents, fathers and parents whose children had been excluded from school. Others who experienced difficulties included parents who weren't fully literate, those who had severe personal problems and those who had difficulties asking for help or in dealing with professionals.[201]

26 Another review found that among the main reasons few parents of teenagers access help were: a lack of opportunities to share experience and swap coping strategies; a sense of embarrassment and stigmatisation about their child's behaviour; a perception that problems experienced by children that age were harder to solve; and a basic lack of appropriate programmes and services.[202]

What is needed?

27 What is needed is a strategic approach to family support, attaching it to other existing services, and focusing on these key transitions where it can be predicted that difficulties might arise.

28 The degree to which the lives of families and young people have changed in the last 20 to 30 years demands a response which takes into account and is targeted on the much longer and more complicated transitions young people need to navigate. None of these transitions is unproblematic, but for many, especially those living in poor neighbourhoods, their premature

or simultaneous occurrence can lead to severe difficulties. The need for support in these areas will be greater.

29 In practice, such targeting could happen through a system of trigger points where agencies could work together to inform family support services when certain transition stages are happening in a young person's life, so that support could be offered. Or information could be targeted by taking transition stages into account, and placing leaflets and information in places where young people going through those transitions – and their parents – are likely to be. This is done in Germany, for example.

30 Targeting support, referral and information to these transitions must not be seen as crisis-intervention. Information must be given in anticipation of the issues likely to be faced following that particular transition, and a background of services which command respect is essential if notice is to be taken of such information.

31 Nor should it be seen as a substitute for the continuing support that some young people (and their families) may need, particularly where they embark on transitions too early or where their lives are suddenly affected by serious events, such as the death of a parent, family breakdown or exclusion from school.

Annex E: Explanatory notes and references to Table 1

1 All figures are for England, unless otherwise stated.

2 Most prevalence figures are under- or low level estimates, usually because the surveys on which they are based under-represent the kinds of respondents who are most likely to fall into the categories of young people covered in the table.

3 Caution needs to be exercised in interpreting trend data. Changes upwards or downwards may reflect changes in a wide range of factors other than the problem itself, such as definitions, thresholds, levels of services, ways of measurement etc.

4 Coincidence of problems in specific at-risk groups should not be taken to infer causality in either direction.

5 International comparisons are fraught with difficulties – often like is not being compared with like – so much of the data in this column should be treated with caution.

6 *Statistical First Release no. 35*, DfEE, 1999.

7 J. Payne *Poor GCSEs: What now?*, PSI, 1999.

8 Ibid.

9 SEU *Bridging the Gap: new opportunities for 16–18 year olds not in education, employment or training* (Cm 4405), TSO, 1999a.

10 J. Sparkes *Schools, Education and Social Exclusion*, CASE paper 29, London School of Economics, 1999.

11 T. Bentley and R. Gurumurthy *Destination Unknown: Engaging with the problems of marginalised youth*, Demos, 1999.

12 H. Glennerster *Tackling poverty at its roots*, IPPR, 1998.

13 *Education across the EU, 1988*, Eurostat, 1998. Note: international comparisons of attainment are complicated by countries having different systems of assessment. The data here uses the International Standard classification of Education, but the results should still be treated with caution.

14 DfEE Statistical First Release 10/99, 1999.

15 *Statistics of Education, Special Educational Needs in England, Statistical Bulletin 12/99*, DfEE, 1999. The rising proportion of children with SEN, whether with or without a statement, may reflect changes other than in objective levels of educational need, such as changes in educational policy and practice or changes in thresholds and definitions of what constitutes need.

16 DfEE Statistical Bulletin, 3/99.

17 DfEE Statistical Bulletin, 9/98.

18 *Sustaining Inclusive Education: Including Students with Special Educational Needs in Mainstream Schools*, OECD, 1999. Note: caution should be exercised in making international comparisons of rates of SEN. Variations are likely to reflect differences in definitions, educational policies and practices and not variations in objective need.

19 *Adult Literacy in Britain*, Office for National Statistics (ONS), 1997.

20 G. Brookes *Trends in standards of literacy in the UK, 1948–1996*, TOPIC, 1998.

21 D. Foxman *Monitoring trends in numeracy in the UK, 1953–1995*, TOPIC, 1998.

22 C. Ekinsmyth and J. Bynner *The Basic skills of Young Adults*, Adult Literacy and Basic Skills Unit, 1994.

23 S. Parsons and J. Bynner *Influences on Adult Basic Skills*, Basic Skills Agency, 1998.

24 R. Carr-Hill, S. Passingham, A. Wolf and N. Kent *Lost Opportunities: the language skills of linguistic minorities in England and Wales*, Basic Skills Agency, 1995.

25 *Report of Working Group chaired by Sir Claus Moser on Improving Literacy and Numeracy*, DfEE, 1999.

26 Youth Cohort Study, *Truancy and Youth Transitions*, 1995.

27 D. J. O'Keefe *Truancy in English Secondary Schools*, 1994. Note: figures likely to be considerable underestimate, since 17 per cent of students not in school when survey took place.

28 Youth Cohort Study *The Activities and Experiences of 16 Year Olds*, 1998.

29 SEU *Truancy and School Exclusion* (Cm 3957), TSO, 1998.

30 J. Graham and B. Bowling *Young People and Crime*, Home Office Research Study no. 145, HMSO, 1995.

31 SEU *Truancy and School Exclusion* (Cm 3957), TSO, 1998b.

32 T. Bentley and R. Gurumurthy op. cit., 1999.

33 SEU op. cit., 1998b.

34 *Missing Out*, Audit Commission, 1999.

35 DfEE Statistics, 1999.

36 *Misspent Youth*, Audit Commission, 1996.

37 SEU op. cit., 1998b.

38 SEU op. cit., 1998b.

39 *Education and Labour Market Status of Young People in England aged 16–18, 1992 to 1998*, DfEE Statistical Bulletin, 11/99, October 1999.

40 SEU op. cit., 1999a.

41 P. Robinson *Education, training and the youth labour market*, in: P. Gregg and J. Wadsworth (editors) *The State of Working Britain*, Manchester University Press, 1999.

42 SEU op. cit., 1999a.

43 *Education at a Glance*, OECD, 1997.

44 ONS *Labour Force Survey 1997/98*, TSO, 1998.

45 ONS *Social Trends 30, 2000 Edition, 2000.*

46 J. Coleman *Key Data on Adolescence*, Trust for the Study of Adolescence, 1999.

47 Ibid.

48 M. Murphy and N. Berrington *Household changes in the 1980s: a review*, Population Trends, 1993.

49 Eurostat.

50 C. Howarth, P. Kenway, G. Palmer and C. Street *Monitoring poverty and social exclusion*, Joseph Rowntree Foundation, 1998.

51 Safe on the Streets Research Team *Still Running: children on the streets in the UK*, The Children's Society, 1999. Note: running away from home is defined as staying away overnight without parents' permission or knowledge.

52 A. Furlong and F. Cartmel *Young People and Social Change*, 1997.

53 C. Howarth, P. Kenway, G. Palmer and C. Street *Monitoring poverty and social exclusion*, Joseph Rowntree Foundation, 1998.

54 G. Jones *Leaving home*, Open University Press, 1995.

55 K. Alexander *Homelessness Factfile 1998/99*, London Research Centre, 1999.

56 *Taking Risks: an analysis of the risks of homelessness for young people in London*, Safe in the City, 1999.

57 A. Furlong and F. Cartmel, op. cit., 1997.

58 Safe on the Streets Research Team *Still Running: children on the streets in the UK*, The Children's Society, 1999.

59 *Youth homelessness in the European Union*, FEANTSA, 1998.

60 A. Walker *Young carers and their families*, Office for National Statistics, 1996.

61 C. Dearden and S. Becker *Young Carers in the United Kingdom: a profile*, National Carers Association, 1998.

62 Ibid.

63 Ibid.

64 Ibid.

65 *Too Much to Take On*, The Princess Royal Trust for Carers, 1999.

66 S. Becker *Young Carers in Europe*, National Carers Association, 1998.

67 Children Act Report, 1995–1999.

68 DH *Children looked after in England: 1998/99*, Statistical Bulletin 1999/26, 1999.

69 Ibid.

70 Ibid.

71 M. Stein *Factsheet on Leaving Care*, Prince's Trust, 1998.

72 Consisting of young people of black African-Caribbean, Asian and mixed racial origin. *Patterns and Outcomes in Child Placement*, DH, 1991

73 SEU *Teenage Pregnancy* (Cm 4342), TSO, 1999b.

74 Ibid.

75 Ibid.

76 Centrepoint, 1999.

77 G. Jones *Leaving home*, Open University Press, 1995.

78 SEU op. cit., 1999b.

79 SEU op. cit., 1999b.

80 ONS *Mortality Statistics by Cause*, DH2, 1998.

81 K. Hawton and J. Fugg *Deliberate self-harm and self-poisoning in adolescence*, British Journal of Psychology, 1992.

82 ONS op. cit., 1998.

83 J. Bynner, E. Ferri and P. Shepherd *Twenty-something in the 1990s*, 1997.

84 ONS op. cit., 1998.

85 J. Bynner, et al, op. cit., 1997.

86 *Children in Mind*, Audit Commission, 1999.

87 T. Craig, S. Hodson, S. Woodward and S. Richardson *Off to a Bad Start*, Mental Health Foundation, 1990.

88 J. Coleman *Key Data on Adolescence*, Trust for the Study of Adolescence, 1999.

89 Ibid.

90 Office of Population Censuses and Surveys (now ONS) *Survey of disability*, TSO, 1989.

91 ONS *Labour Force Survey Autumn 1999*, TSO, 1999.

92 Office of Population Censuses and Surveys (now ONS) *Survey of disability*, TSO, 1989.

93 This may in part reflect the fact that disabilities are more easily identified once a child begins school. Office of Population Censuses and Surveys (now ONS) *Survey of disability*, TSO, 1989.

94 M. Ramsay and S. Partridge *Drug Misuse Declared in 1998: Results from the British Crime Survey*, Home Office Research Study No. 197, 1999.

95 Heroin, methadone, cocaine, crack.

96 Amphetamines, LSD, magic mushrooms, ecstasy and poppers.

97 *British Crime Survey*, HO, 1998.

98 *Annual report on the state of the drugs problem in the European Union*, EMCDDA, 1998.

99 ONS *Health Statistics Quarterly, Volume 5: drugs-related deaths database: first results for England and Wales, 1993–1997*, 2000

100 J. Balding *Young People and Illegal Drugs in 1998*, J. Exeter: Scholl, Health Education Unit.

101 J. Balding *Young People in 1999*, J. Exeter: Scholl, Health Education Unit.

102 *Drug Misuse Declared in 1998: Results from the British Crime Survey*, 1999. Note: some of these percentages are based on small numbers and should therefore be treated with caution.

103 *British Crime Survey*, HO, 1996.

104 H. Parker, F. Measham and J. Aldridge *Drugs Futures: changing patterns of drug use amongst English youth*, ISDD, 1995.

105 The higher rate of cocaine use among young men is based on small numbers and should be treated with caution.

106 SEU op. cit., 1998b.

107 *Drug Misuse Declared in 1998: results from the British Crime Survey*, 1999.

108 H. Parker, C. Bury and R. Egginton *New Heroin Outbreaks amongst Young People in England and Wales*, HO, 1998.

109 M. Leitner, J. Shapland and P. Wiles *Drug Usage and Drugs Prevention*, 1993.

110 EMCDDA op. cit., 1998.

111 *British Crime Survey*, HO, 1996.

112 H. Meltzer, B. Gill and M Petticrew *The Prevalance of Psychiatric Morbidity among Adults aged 16–64 living in Private Households in Great Britain*, OPCS, 1995.

113 E. Goddard and V. Higgins *Smoking, Drinking and Drug Use among Young Teenagers in 1998*, Volume 1, ONS, 1999.

114 ONS *Living in Britain: results from the 1996 General Household Survey*, 1998.

115 Alcohol Concern *Proposals for a National Alcohol Strategy for England*, 1999.

116 HO, 1993 *Youth Lifestyles Survey*, unpublished.

117 E. Goddard and V. Higgins op. cit., 1999.

118 E. Goddard and V. Higgins op. cit., 1999.

119 Ibid.

120 Ibid.

121 World Health Organization, Regional Office for Europe *Health and health behaviour among young people,* WHP Policy Series, *Health Policy for Children and Adolescents,* Issue 1, forthcoming.

122 C. Mirrlees-Black, T. Budd, S. Partridge and P. Mayhew *The 1998 British Crime Survey,* Home Office Statistical Bulletin 21/98, GSS, 1999.

123 C. Mirrlees-Black *Domestic Violence: findings from a new British Crime Survey self-completed questionnaire, no. 191*, 1999.

124 J. Graham and B. Bowling *Young People and Crime,* Home Office Research Study no.145, TSO,1995.

125 N. Aye-Maung *Young People, Victimisation and the Police,* Home Office Research Study no. 140, TSO, 1995.

126 N. Madge *Abuse and Survival: A fact file,* The Prince's Trust, 1997.

127 C. Mirrlees-Black et al, op. cit., 1999.

128 N. Madge *Abuse and Survival: A fact file,* The Prince's Trust, 1997.

129 C. Mirrlees-Black et al, op. cit., 1999.

130 P. Mayhew, P. and J.J. van Dijk *Criminal Victimisation in Eleven Industrialised Countries: Key findings from the 1996 International Crime Victim Survey,* 1997. Countries included: Netherlands, England and Wales, USA, Canada, France, Scotland, Sweden, Switzerland, Finland, Austria and Northern Ireland.

131 *Criminal Careers of those born between 1953 and 1973,* Home Office Statistical Bulletin 14/95, 1995.

132 Home Office, *Home Office Digest: information on the criminal justice system in England and Wales,* 1999.

133 Ibid.

134 J. Graham and B. Bowling, op. cit., 1995.

135 R. Hood *Home Office Research Study No. 180*, 1992.

136 *Misspent Youth*, Audit Commission, 1996.

137 C. Pfeiffer *Juvenile Crime and Juvenile Violence in European Countries*, Kriminologisches Forschungs Institut, 1997.

138 Prison Statistics, England and Wales, TSO, 1999.

139 Ibid.

140 Home Office, *Home Office Digest: information on the criminal justice system in England and Wales,* 1999.

141 Prison Statistics, op. cit., 1999.

142 *Young prisoners: a thematic review of HM Chief Inspector of Prisons for England and Wales,* HO, 1997.

143 *SPACE 97.1*, Council of Europe, 1997. Note: no data available for Albania, Bulgaria, Denmark, Germany, Greece, Latvia, Luxembourg, Malta, Moldova and the Ukraine.

Annex F: Policy map

Area of young person's life: Family structure | Family employment/income | Learning and employment | Leisure and lifestyle | Health | Drugs and alcohol | Crime | Leaving home/starting a family

Targets

- **Learning and employment:**
  - Get 250,000 18–24s off welfare into work by end of this Parliament (DfEE)
  - All 16–19s proficient in oral and written communication, application of number and IT (DfEE)
  - Reduce truancy/exclusion by one-third, ensure excluded pupils receive full-time education, by 2002 (DfEE)
- **Health:** Halve the rate of conception by under-18s by 2010 (DH)
- **Drugs and alcohol:** Ensure all children receive good drug education; better inform parents and teachers; ensure young people most at risk of developing serious drug problems receive appropriate help and advice (CO)
- **Crime:** Halve the time from arrest to sentence for persistent young offenders (HO)
- **Leaving home/starting a family:** Reduce number of people sleeping rough throughout England to a third of its current level by 2002 (DETR)

Policies

- **Family structure:** Supporting Families (HO)
- **Family employment/income:**
  - Working Families' Tax Credit (HMT)
  - Annual report on reducing poverty (DSS)
  - Minimum Wage (DTI)
- **Learning and employment:**
  - New Deal for young people (DfEE)
  - Key Skills (DfEE)
  - Truancy and Exclusion (DfEE)
  - FE funding changes (DfEE)
- **Leisure and lifestyle:** National Sports Strategy (DCMS)
- **Health:**
  - Teenage pregnancy (DH)
  - Modernising Social Services (DH)
  - Care Leavers (DH)
- **Drugs and alcohol:** Drugs Strategy (CO)
- **Crime:**
  - Youth Justice Reforms, including YJB and YOTs (HO)
  - Juvenile Secure Estate/Young Offenders in Custody (HO)
- **Leaving home/starting a family:**
  - Rough sleepers (DETR)
  - Housing Policy Green Paper (DETR)

Initiatives

- Quality Protects (DH) – spans Family employment/income to Crime
- Review of maintenance for 16–17s (LCD)
- Learning Gateway for 16–17s (DfEE)
- Right to time off for study or training (DfEE)
- Initial Teacher Training (DfEE)
- Child and Adolescent Mental Health Services (DH)
- Alcohol Strategy (HO)
- ParentLine Plus (HO)
- ConneXions Service (DfEE) – spans Learning and employment to Leaving home/starting a family
- Family Support Grant (HO)
- Education Maintenance Allowance pilots (HMT)
- New Start (DfEE)
- Youth Inclusion Programme for high risk teenagers (HO/YJB)
- National Family and Parenting Institute (HO)
- Education Action Zones (DfEE)
- Study Support (DfEE)
- Millennium Volunteers (DfEE)
- On Track – multiple intervention programme (HO) – spans Family employment/income to Crime
- Youth Card (DfEE)
- New Audiences programme (DCMS)
- Dialogue with Young People (HO/CO) – spans Family employment/income to Leaving home/starting a family

Plans

- Education Development Plan (DfEE)
- Behaviour Support Plan (DfEE)
- Special Educational Needs Plans (DfEE)
- Children's Services Plans (DH)
- Youth Justice Plans (HO)

Key:
- CO – Cabinet Office
- DfEE – Department for Education and Employment
- DTI – Department of Trade and Industry
- LCD – Lord Chancellor's Department
- DCMS – Department for Culture, Media and Sport
- DH – Department of Health
- HMT – HM Treasury
- YJB – Youth Justice Board
- DETR – Department of the Environment, Transport and the Regions
- DSS – Department of Social Security
- HO – Home Office

Annex G: Co-ordination for youth in other European countries

1 Research undertaken in 1998 for the Youth Directorate of the Council of Europe looked at youth policy and legislation in countries which were party to the Cultural Convention of the Council of Europe. The report of this work[203] shows that over a third of those surveyed had an identified 'Minister for Youth', and half a single department, ministry or committee with an overarching responsibility for young people. These departments, and where present the Ministers for Youth within them, typically also had responsibility for sports, culture and social affairs.

2 The table below shows what kind of co-ordinating mechanism countries in the European Union have:

Country	Minister for Youth[204]	Ministry for Youth[205]	Parliamentary Committee[206]	Cross-government youth policy[207]
Austria	■	■		■
Belgium	■[208]	■		■
Denmark				
Finland	■	■	[209]	■
France	■	■		■
Germany	■	■	■	■
Greece		■		
Ireland	■	■		■
Italy	■	■		[210]
Luxembourg	■	■	■	■
Netherlands		■	■	
Portugal	■	■	■	■
Spain	■		■	■
Sweden	■	■	■	■
UK				

3 In the countries identified as having youth policies, the common elements seem to be:

- social cohesion between Government, young people and society through consultation and involvement;
- advice and information on young people's rights and the opportunities available to them;
- freedom of cultural, creative and political expression;
- a culture of continuous education and training;
- support for young families;
- appropriate specialised assistance for young people 'at risk' such as those with disabilities or young offenders;
- support for and promotion of leisure activities;
- the right training for those working with young people;
- research on the difficulties facing young people; and
- fostering international relations between young people.

4 Countries use different institutional arrangements to achieve these goals. Examples from France, Germany, Sweden and Portugal are shown below:

Missions Locales, France

Missions Locales are youth training centres which provide a place for young people aged 16–25 to meet, discuss and resolve problems associated with employment, training, finance and, in some cases, accommodation with professional experts. Many are unemployed and/or unqualified school leavers. The *Missions* uses its contacts to help to find places on training schemes, and offers courses in literacy and numeracy and advice on applying for temporary and permanent employment.

An important principle of the *Missions Locales* is to help young people develop projects themselves. Grants are available for starting up enterprises and any young people, provided they are not in employment, can propose a project and apply for funding with the help of *Missions* staff. Projects are discussed informally by a special committee. If approved, they are then submitted to the local crime prevention council with a recommendation for partial or full finance. Projects such as multi-racial theatre workshops, dance parties, sports clubs and camping and study holidays have been funded.

Missions Locales are locally based, with contact to professional workers and employers and their own broadly based management committee. This includes local representatives from trade unions, government departments, trade councils and the voluntary sector. Half of the funding is generated locally, half from central government.

Germany

Institutions
One of the main features of services for children and young people in Germany is the prominent role played by the voluntary support agencies. In many fields of youth work, the voluntary sector provides most services and facilities.

The main input from the statutory sector comes from the youth services, which operate at four levels:

- at *federal* level, through the Federal Ministry for Women and Youth, preparing legislation and financing initiatives and best practice models (all under the Children and Youth Plan of the Federation);
- at the *state* level, by preparing legislation for each federal state, providing support for projects and developing youth services;
- at the *regional* level, through the regional Youth Offices, performing advisory, co-ordinating, regional planning and training functions; and
- at the *local* level, through the local Youth Offices (currently 700), making decisions on individual cases relating to care and guardianship.

Youth policy
The aims of federal youth policy are:

- to promote the personal and social development of children and young people;
- to counter any negative influences upon them by supporting parents and other legal guardians in their educational role;
- to provide greater opportunities for their development and education; and
- to ensure that living and environmental conditions are geared to the needs of children and families.

The Federal Government pursues these goals through focusing on:

- voluntary work;
- prevention and control of juvenile crime;
- combating youth unemployment; and
- combating the sexual exploitation of children.

As part of the evaluation procedure for this, a group of independent researchers submits a report to the two chambers of parliament every session on the situation of children and young people in Germany. This includes an assessment of the work done and results achieved by the Youth Offices. These reports also contain proposals for further action.

Sweden

Institutions

In 1986 a Cabinet Minister – the Minister for Youth Affairs – was for the first time given specific responsibility for youth-related issues, along with other issues such as integration, gender equality and sports. Youth issues are co-ordinated by a central unit which since the end of 1998 has been situated in the Ministry of Culture.

The Government's commitment to a co-ordinated youth policy is made clear in the rules governing the joint handling of measures, which state:

> *"Government matters of special importance to young people and their living conditions are handled in co-operation with the unit dealing with issues pertaining to non-governmental organisations and youth policy."*

The National Board for Youth Affairs, a government body, studies the living, training and employment conditions of young people and evaluates and advises on the way youth policy is put into practice at central and local government level. The National Board will also provide advice on youth-related projects to the Inheritance Fund Delegation, which oversees the distribution of funds from the National Inheritance Fund.

Youth involvement

Legislative and other social reforms are prepared not only by the ministries but also by Inquiry Commissions, set up by the Government to look at specific issues. Representatives of interest groups, including young people, often participate in this work, and all organisations have a right to submit their views. For example, commissions have looked at:

- age limits – looking at the effect of such limits on those aged under 30; this had an expert panel consisting of representatives from different youth organisations;

- youth policies – looking at the goals of youth policy, and made up of young politicians from parties in Parliament; and

- the IT Youth Council, looking at how children and young people could use information technology, involved only children and young people as participants in its work.

Legislation

Swedish legislation does not include any laws relating specifically to young people. The Social Service Act states that the municipal authorities must create the necessary conditions for the development and personal growth of children and young people.

Sweden has ratified the United Nations Convention on the Rights of the Child. In 1993 the Government created a post of ombudsman for children's rights to supervise application of the Convention's provisions.

Funding

At national level the National Board for Youth Affairs distributes grants and subsidies to those youth organisations which have a national membership. Special subsidies are granted to sports organisations whose members are mainly young people.

Portugal

Institution
Responsibility for youth affairs rests with one of two State Secretaries from the Ministry of Youth Affairs, Sport and Drug Abuse.

The Portuguese Youth Affairs Institute is the main body responsible for Government youth policy, carrying out this task through:

- keeping in contact with a range of youth organisations;
- giving financial and technical support to youth-related projects;
- encouraging young people to work in community and international bodies; and
- devising and implementing programmes to support young people.

Youth policy
One of the key aims of the Government is to encourage youth participation and promote young people's social and economic integration into society. This is being carried forward through:

- the implementation of a cross-cutting youth policy in collaboration with other ministries; and
- ensuring this policy is integrated from the Government level down to the individual, promoting youth participation, freedom of creative expression and the spread of information.

The main strands of the policy centre on:

- enhancing Government dialogue with young people;
- supporting and encouraging young people's decision-making ability;
- promoting exchanges and co-operation with other young people;
- supporting the fight against drugs; and
- supporting and promoting leisure activities.

Annex H: Explanatory notes to Table 4

1 These figures are based upon S. Scott, M. Knapp, J. Henderson and B. Maughan *The price of social exclusion: the cost of anti-social children grown up*, Final Report to the Mental Health Foundation, 1999. Based on the work of Rutter et al, this predicts a prevalence of conduct disorder amongst children of four to eight per cent. The calculations take the lower figure, so represent a range of possible values up to twice those shown. The calculations are based on the average additional expenditure to the age of 27 of a group of young people diagnosed as having conduct disorders at the age of ten (compared to those with a diagnosis at ten of 'no problems').

2 DfEE, Statistical Release SFR 11/1999.

3 Each young person in alternative education costs at least an additional £1,800; the cost of a place in a Pupil Referral Unit (PRU) is £4,300 compared with £2,500 for a place in mainstream education. This figure is the result of a number of simplifications – the number of permanently excluded pupils placed in PRUs is in reality about a third – a further third are found alternative provision. This also 'double counts' those who are permanently excluded on more than one occasion. Both of these factors serve to reduce the actual cost. However, the unit cost quoted does not cover year-on-year provision for those permanently excluded well before Year 11 – the additional annual cost of a continuing permanent exclusion is higher, at around £2,600 per young person: see C. Parsons *Exclusion from School: the public cost*, Commission for Racial Equality, 1996.

4 Home Office research suggests around 60 per cent of those excluded from school go on to become young offenders – in fact the cautioned and/or convicted figure may be higher. The NACRO report *Wasted Lives* (1998) estimates the average response cost in dealing with the behaviour of a young offender to be around £52,000 (made up of prosecution, incarceration and supervision costs as well as family intervention and care).

5 M. Liddle in *Wasted Lives: counting the cost of juvenile offending* (NACRO/The Prince's Trust, 1998) estimates the direct costs of offending to others to average around £22,700 per young offender.

6 A variety of research studies have attempted to estimate the percentage of the population who are regular drug users (see, for example, M. Ramsay and S. Partridge *Drug Misuse Declared in 1998: results from the British Crime Survey*), and it seems generally accepted that no more than one per cent of the population have used heroin in the last year. This does not of course suggest that all of these people are problem drug users, so in this respect the figure used is probably an *overestimate*. However, all surveys work on self-reporting, which is known to considerably underestimate the true figures of problem drug misuse. It is not possible to say to what extent one effect balances out the other.

7 It is estimated that the average heroin user generates around £13,500 per year in illegally earned income. Further analysis suggests this can be broken down as follows: acquisitive crime 65 per cent; drug dealing 12 per cent; combination of the two 23 per cent.

8 Research commissioned for the SEU's *Bridging the Gap* report (TSO, 1999a) looked at the effects at 21 for those young people who had not participated for six months or more during this period (around six per cent of the cohort, or around 107,000 young people).

9 Young men who did not participate for six months or more experienced unemployment rates at 21 of around 44 per cent, young women of around 68 per cent. (In fact for young women the definition was 'not in full- or part-time employment'.) Taking a 50:50 split between the sexes of the numbers of young people in the 'six months of non-participation' category, this might suggest some 60,000 of these young people are unemployed at 21, at a potential annual cost in benefits paid of £3,800 per person.

10 Potential annual contributions lost each year per person are around £4,400.

11 Research for the *Bridging the Gap* report also suggests that some 60 per cent of young women who had not participated for six months or more between 16 and 18 years would become teenage parents, around 32,000 (although there will clearly be substantial double counting with those young women in the unemployed category). The SEU's *Teenage Pregnancy* report (TSO, 1999b) noted that a mother aged 16–17 can claim between £65 and £75 per week in Income Support.

12 The *Bridging the Gap* report states that the average weekly wage for an employed 16–18 year old is £137.20.

Annex I: Best practice case studies

Fairbridge

Fairbridge has 11 centres, based in some of the UK's most deprived inner cities. It offers young people a long-term personal development programme enabling them to develop the self-esteem and skills they need to meet the opportunities and responsibilities of modern society. Provision is tailored to individual needs and combines practical activities with long-term support.

Young people who go to Fairbridge are often characterised by a failure to make commitments or to see things through. Last year 1,600 disaffected young people stuck with it and finished a week-long 'basic' induction course.

Young people participated in a wide range of life skill courses, achieving thousands of personal goals such as learning to cook healthily and cheaply, getting involved in local community groups or learning about what to expect in the workplace. Acquiring these skills motivated them to make significant changes to their lifestyles. For example, young people found secure accommodation, got back in touch with their family or stayed off drugs.

Fairbridge operates in some of the worst unemployment blackspots in the country, but last year more than 270 young people moved on from their programme directly into a job. Almost twice that number progressed towards employment by moving onto further education, vocational training or a personal development programme with another youth organisation.

Impact
More than 120 young people returned to school despite exclusion or a history of persistent truanting.

Over 230 got more involved in their local community through voluntary work.

Evaluation
A recent Home Office study concluded that the Venture Trust Project, run by Fairbridge for young offenders, significantly reduces reoffending rates.

Youthstart 2000, Birmingham

Run by the city council's Youth and Community Team, this project is aimed at groups of disaffected young people in poor neighbourhoods of the city.

It uses technology imaginatively to motivate young people to learn. They become competent in digital photography/imaging, videoconferencing, using the Internet, DTP/graphic design, software design, using interactive music and computer-generated music. Each individual is involved in creating their own web site. They have also produced a CD-ROM 'Driving Your Life' designed by young people for young people offering information and advice on common problems and challenges facing young people in urban areas. Young people get Open College Network accreditation for learning and achievement on programmes.

Safe in the City

The Safe in the City partnership programme aims: to help young people stay safely at home; to find alternative options for young people who cannot remain safely at home; and to develop the life skills and employability of young people to enable them to make a smooth transition to independent lifestyles.

The programme is delivered through a partnership of statutory and voluntary agencies in eight participating boroughs. Projects which are funded through the programme include: estate-based centres; family counselling and family mediation services; mentoring and peer education projects; training and life skills programmes; respite hostel beds; and support projects for young runaways.

A research report commissioned as part of the programme has provided practical guidance for each borough partnership on the factors that lead to youth homelessness, and is being used to develop a composite measure of the risk of homelessness among young people in London.

Daytime Potentials, Derby

Based at Derby House, a youth project in the city centre, this serves young adults across the city but particularly those in poor neighbourhoods such as Chaddesden.

It uses effective group work to build confidence and personal skills in parenting, job search, mental health and other everyday life challenges, moving on to more structured programmes so young people can gain qualifications in IT, health and safety, key skills and vocational skills such as fork-lift driving. It has developed an imaginative 'Wheels and Words' project linking driving and literacy and uses a lot of peer mentoring. The driving force behind this scheme was herself one of the city's most disaffected some years ago.

Peer Tutoring Project, Newcastle upon Tyne

This is a project that has evolved from the most successful Career Clubs run by Tyneside Careers. Funded by DfEE and the local Training and Enterprise Council (TEC), the Careers Service trains and co-ordinates graduates from Career Clubs to go into schools and youth groups to run workshops and provide support for Key Stage 3 youngsters who are at risk of some of the same problems they have faced – educational failure, unemployment, homelessness, drug abuse and offending. Twenty-four young people have been peer tutors in the last 18 months and some have moved on to further education and work. They give their time voluntarily and derive considerable self-esteem from doing something of value for others.

Adolescent Sexuality and Pregnancy Prevention Programme, Children's Aid Society, New York

Set up in 1985, the programme works by integrating sexuality and family life education with academic support, career training, health care, counselling, sports and a guarantee of admission to college for every young person (or their parent) who completes the programme. It starts at age 12 and can continue past high school, giving young people compelling alternatives to pregnancy and the tools to achieve their goals. Currently operating in 20 states, the programme is run on a franchise basis, with community leaders who express an interest in developing a programme in their area being provided with the necessary training and support.

Programme content – there are five main activities in each programme:

- education – including homework clubs, intensive tutoring and extra lessons;
- career guidance and job training – including practical, paid, work experience;
- art and drama – developing the creative talents of young people;
- family life and sex education – age-appropriate sexuality education; and
- sport – building discipline and self-control through individual sports.

In addition, all the young people receive free, high-quality medical care, access to mental health specialists and general health care advice.

Intensity – the programme operates six days a week, young people arrive straight from school and stay for between two and five hours depending on their age. All the programmes have an active outreach element so those who 'default' on the programme can be quickly encouraged to rejoin.

Participants – those encouraged to join are young people who have all the indicators for future failure such as poor school attainment, and who often have families where substance abuse and violence are common. The young people often come from communities where there is little experience of regular employment. Stipends are earned by all young people through the Employment Program (usually every two weeks), on the condition that they open a bank account – a further aid to developing their future.

Location – the Children's Aid Society has developed and helped implement 12 programmes in New York and 33 programmes in other cities in the USA. They are based in existing community facilities such as youth clubs or leisure centres, and are all financed from private donations. Although the programme is similar to 'after-school' clubs, it does not directly involve schools.

Parents – are closely involved with all stages of the programme. Parents must enter into a contract with the programme providers to enable their children to participate. Parents are encouraged to attend at least once a month. There are opportunities for discussions between workers and parents on talking to their children about sexuality, as well as ongoing meetings and personal support. The community workers employed by the programme are fundamental in carrying out this work with parents.

Evaluation

Two separate evaluations have shown that young people involved in the programme stay in school longer, delay sexual activity longer and attend college at higher rates than their peers. Compared to the US teenage pregnancy average of around one in ten, those leaving the programme have only a one in 25 risk of teenage pregnancy.

The Strathmore Centre, London

The Centre is a joint initiative between the Social Services and Education Departments of the London Borough of Richmond upon Thames. The Centre provides:

- full-time education for Year 11 pupils excluded from school, under a supervision order or out of school for some other reason; and
- one-to-one in-school support and group work for 'at risk' young people referred to them by the school or social services.

The Centre also now houses the YOT.

The Centre's general objectives include:

- reducing reoffending;
- improving young people's self-image and self-worth; and
- helping young people get back into and stay in school by achieving a more regular and consistent pattern of behaviour and attendance.

Impact
Last year, of 16 young people on the full-time educational programme:

- the Centre achieved an average of 79 per cent attendance record, in a context where over 44 per cent of the group had not been to school for the previous 12 months;
- 93 per cent of pupils took between two and five AEB and RSA examinations, achieving a 75 per cent pass rate. Twelve per cent took two GCSEs and obtained passes;
- 82 per cent obtained a college place, training or vocational course or employment upon leaving the Centre; and
- 37 per cent had committed an offence prior to attending the Centre. Only one committed a further offence whilst attending the Centre.

A questionnaire of young people using the Centre showed that:

- 80 per cent found the information they received about the aims of the Centre and their progress very good;
- 66 per cent felt the Centre had a positive impact on their general behaviour;
- 90 per cent felt the Centre had a very positive impact on their career opportunities; and
- 62 per cent felt that the Centre had been 'very good' in meeting agreed aims and objectives.

Base 51, Nottingham

This is a multi-agency health care project in Nottingham city centre.

It provides information, advice and counselling as well as practical services like creche, subsidised meals and pregnancy testing. A good example of local authority and voluntary sector partnership, it serves all young people but is especially used by those who are homeless and vulnerable. Clients get advice on welfare and employment matters as well as health. It provides a mixture of crisis intervention and longer-term projects, and seeks to provide holistic responses to what may be presented as single-issue problems.

42nd Street, Manchester

For 18 years this project has been providing an unusual combination of mental health and youth work.

Most common approaches are role-play and discussion groups as well as creative activities such as making a video or producing a magazine. It brings in teachers, social workers and community nurses to provide a range of perspectives and skills on young people's problems. It is involved in Outreach work with schools and youth groups in community venues.

Sosjale Joenits, The Netherlands

In the Netherlands, some 60 youth advisory centres – *Sosjales Joenits* – exist throughout the country. They offer advice and support to young people between 11 and 25 (though mostly between 16 and 20) on matters relating to housing, employment, education, training, social security, and drugs and alcohol problems. They adopt a child-centred approach, work closely with the police and target their resources in particular on runaways, the unemployed, the homeless and other young people at risk.

They are concerned with helping young people to help themselves so that, for example, runaways who come to the centres for accommodation are required to participate in a survival skills training course before they are accepted in hostels. The emphasis is on teaching young people how to make decisions for themselves and live with the consequences, and how to gain self-confidence and self-esteem.

The Dutch youth centres adopt the approach of trying to integrate young people into a society or community from which they feel estranged or rejected.

Communities that Care (UK)

Communities that Care (UK) is a long-term programme for building safer neighbourhoods where children and young people are valued, respected and encouraged to achieve their potential.

The programme establishes a working partnership between local people, agencies and organisations to promote healthy personal and social development among young people, while reducing the risks of different problem behaviours.

It applies knowledge about the factors most likely to encourage self-motivation, achievement and social commitment among young people.

The programme leads to local action plans in which the principal goals are to:

- support and strengthen families;
- promote school commitment and success;
- encourage responsible sexual behaviour; and
- achieve a safer, more cohesive community.

The programme is based on research that has shown that there are influential risk factors in children's lives that increase their chances of developing health and behaviour problems as they grow older. Equally importantly, there are protective factors that help to shield young people from problems. Using a step-by-step approach, Communities that Care makes it possible to map factors in the lives of local children that are making it more – or less – likely they will experience:

- school failure; and
- school age pregnancy and sexually transmitted diseases;

or become involved in:

- drug abuse;
- violence; and
- crime.

Analysis of the particular risks influencing children in the neighbourhood leads to a strategy where genuine priorities can be targeted for action. Informed decisions can then be taken about existing services and the most effective way of applying them. Gaps in provision can also be identified and filled by introducing new interventions as necessary.

This ensures that the final plan of action is rooted in knowledge of best and most effective practice, including a menu of 'promising approaches' which are existing prevention programmes that have a track record of success in reducing risks and increasing protection.

continued...

Communities that Care (UK) (continued)

The programme involves four main stages:

- community involvement;
- risk and resources audit;
- action planning and implementation; and
- monitoring and evaluation.

Programmes currently under way in Barnsley, Swansea and Coventry are at the action planning and implementation stage. Eight further areas are being established and will carry out risk audits by early in 2000. Whilst there has therefore not as yet been any evaluation of the process in the UK, Communities that Care is being widely implemented in the USA with Federal Government support.

Barnardo's, Freagarrach Project, Scotland

A community-based project working with around 20, 12–16 year old persistent young offenders at a time (nearly 100 over the course of a year). The project is staffed by people with backgrounds in social work or in youth and community work, but is thought to benefit from being in the voluntary sector. It is therefore not associated with a fear of 'social workers'.

The project aims to:

- challenge offending behaviour;
- raise awareness of the impact of crime and offer opportunities for reparation;
- support educational involvement so as to maximise potential through education, training and employment;
- encourage and help parents and carers to provide appropriate levels of care and control; and
- encourage young people to make a constructive use of leisure pursuits.

The project involves a mixture of individual work, group work programmes and work with families. Referral is by consent of the young person, and family members are also expected to co-operate and sign a contract to attend. Each young person is attached to a key worker and usually stays with this person for the duration of their involvement in the project (typically ten months).

The project has a reoffending rate of under 40 per cent (at a cost of £330 per young person per week), compared to a nearby Secure Training Centre, where reoffending rates are almost 100 per cent (£2,400).

SSP (School, Social Services, Police) Committees, Denmark

In Denmark, 230 out of 275 municipalities have SSP Committees. Policy, decision-making and resource allocation affecting young people are determined by a Parent Committee, usually comprising the chairs of education, social services and the police.

Each Parent Committee has a number of permanent working parties comprising social workers, teachers and police officers. These meet regularly to discuss trends, specific problems and referred cases. Every school in the municipality has a contact person who is responsible for liaison with the working party.

A permanent working party can set up a provisional or temporary task force to combat specific problems, for example, sudden increases in shoplifting in the city centre or the misuse of drugs in a specific youth club. Membership of these varies according to the problem being tackled, but may include, in addition to police officers, social workers and teachers, people such as retailers, youth workers and parents.

The principles underpinning the SSP approach are:

- continuity of intervention – particularly between school moves (nursery – infants – primary – secondary); and
- involving parents – if only by making them aware of what their children are up to. Parents are seen as an important source of information on their children's use of leisure time and their performance and behaviour in school.

Impact
While no quantitative data is yet available as to how successful the SSP approach is in tackling crime and fear of crime, much has been written about the ability of SSP committee members to work effectively together. It is also clear that there has been a real change of attitude over a period of the last 20 years. This has involved the acceptance of professional differences and the breaking down of the stereotypes participating agencies had of one another, and a recognition of how each profession has different qualities that can be effectively harnessed by good teamwork.

Vietnamese Community Association of Western Australia (VCAWA)

The VCAWA is a voluntary organisation providing advice, information and other support to the Vietnamese community, as well as organising key community and religious celebrations (70 per cent are Buddhists).

By the mid-1990s the VCAWA was becoming concerned about the involvement of local young people in alcohol and drug misuse, and in crime and imprisonment, educational underachievement and truancy. Most were aged 13–18 and in conflict with their parents, who disapproved of their adoption of western culture and failure to meet high academic expectations.

The VCAWA had had little contact with these 'at risk' young people, who were equally isolated from their non-Vietnamese peers. It sought to overcome this, and the general distrust these young people had for professionals in general, by entering into agreement with a local youth agency to employ a Vietnamese youth worker. Both organisations, together with another local youth project, worked to develop a multi-agency strategy, involving the local Youth Affairs Council and the police.

It was agreed that the police would initially adopt a low profile, and that to maximise participation, the project would centre on initiatives which would:

- provide advocacy support;
- promote recreational activities;
- challenge criminal, in particular violent, behaviour; and
- improve employment, education and training opportunities.

Impact
Within six months of its implementation, the project was already showing signs of success. Contact with marginalised young Vietnamese people had increased dramatically. Typically the project worked with groups of up to 20 young men on a weekly basis, and by the end of this initial period more than half of each group had enrolled in training courses or found employment.

The value of the Vietnamese youth worker – and of a second later employed by the project – was found in developing close links with the young people and representing their views to the local police, as well as reducing conflict between them and other non-Vietnamese communities. The knowledge gained by the youth worker also allowed the VCAWA to better target their services, resulting in an increase in uptake. It also in turn allowed the VCAWA to better articulate their own service needs to the voluntary sector and to local and central government.

Oldham Youth and Community Service: Buzz Project and Transitions Into Work

These are two different projects aimed at supporting young people in poor neighbourhoods to orient themselves to learning and work.

The Buzz project is a partnership between the Youth Service and the Careers Service. A bus, equipped with information and computers, goes on to the estates, and youth workers and careers advisers provide young people with one-to-one advice and information.

The Transitions Into Work project is aimed at care leavers who need support in finding their way into training and work. Funded by the European Social Fund (ESF), the programme consists of 13-week courses designed to build self-confidence and decision-making skills through profiling, information and advice, and group work. The Careers Service works closely with social services and the Youth Service to organise carefully matched work experience placements as a much-valued part of the programme.

Acorn Initiative, North Nottinghamshire

Serving the depressed coalfields area of North Nottinghamshire.

Run by the local authority Youth and Community Service and supported by various funding streams, Acorn provides support and training for young people mainly aged 16-plus who cannot find work or are not attracted to conventional education and training opportunities. It has established sound working partnerships with Further Education Colleges, TECs, the Careers Service and training providers.

It has just won a contract to provide the life skills option on the Learning Gateway, and also runs a mentoring scheme for New Deal Gateway clients. It uses a mixture of one-to-one and group work, is community-based, and tailors provision to individual needs. It co-ordinates strategy across agencies to prevent scheme-hopping.

Winner of first Young Adult Learners Award.

Leeds City Council

Leeds City Council has created a single claim form for an entire range of benefits – from free school meals to housing benefit and school clothing grants – and to connect this information to records of pupil achievement.

This allows analysis of educational progress in relation to socio-economic circumstances of the family. It can therefore rank different schools in terms of which pupils are from disadvantaged backgrounds. The data generated has provided firm evidence of the links between those schools with large numbers receiving benefits and low GCSE performance. This information has been used in a variety of ways including:

- analysis of 'value added' in schools;
- analysis of the extent to which children of lone parents are receiving necessary support;
- tracing the extent to which FE colleges and Leeds University are widening participation;
- refocusing the work of the Youth Service in accordance with the patterns of risk and need;
- securing additional funding and planning regeneration initiatives; and
- community planning and needs analysis, and analysis of local crime.

Neighbourhood Youth Team, Bradford

The Youth Team programme has been developed to train and equip a team of ten–12 young people aged 18–25 years, who will work full time in one or more of the SRB areas in Bradford, undertaking crime prevention and regeneration work with individuals and groups. Discussions focusing on crime prevention with local communities, agencies and the local authority identified the need for young people to act as young role models/peer educators/mentors in these areas. Members of the team will have local knowledge of the communities in which they will be working and will follow a two-year training course.

The training course includes:

- personal development;
- interpersonal skills;
- into employment techniques;
- crime and drug prevention; and
- health, housing and environment issues.

The scheme is part of a local authority strategy to prevent youth crime, and crucial to this will be the recruitment of young people who have lived the reality of social conditions in the inner city and on disadvantaged estates. They will be able to respond effectively to the needs of the communities as peer mentors and role models. So far, two teams of young people have started the programme (32 people in total) – one of which is working on outer estates and one in the inner city in Bradford. Programmes are also being delivered out of school for young people – for example, a health programme for girls aged eight–15.

Evaluation
The University of Bradford has been commissioned to produce an evaluation of the programme. The following aspects will be evaluated:

- the impact of the programme on Youth Team members;
- the impact on young people aged eight–21 who engage with the Youth Team; and
- the impact on the local community.

Aberdeen Youth Strategy

Aberdeen City Council's Youth Strategy sets out the authority's intentions for improving the provision of services for young people and for more effectively involving young people in community life.

Preparation of the Strategy was undertaken by a working group whose discussions were informed by a Youth Action Committee. Membership was drawn from young people involved in youth projects across the city. The Strategy was prepared after:

- reviewing services provided for young people, both by the city council and other agencies;
- workshop discussions with the Youth Action Committee and representatives of youth agencies; and
- consideration of recommendations from three task groups, focusing on: employment and training; crime; and participation and consultation.

Following consultation on a draft document, the Strategy proper was issued early this year. The Strategy is targeted on young people aged 16–25 years, also considering linkages with younger teenagers and with the Council's Children's Strategy (0–16 years). Its aims are:

- *co-ordination:* create links between all the different services for young people;
- *participation:* encourage young people to get involved in their community;
- *equal opportunities:* support new work to tackle inequality and widen opportunities for young people; and
- *a voice:* set up representative groups which give a public voice for young people.

Amongst issues identified as important during the development of the Strategy were:

- support at times of change such as leaving school, family break-up and leaving care/home;
- access to lifelong learning;
- information about services, issues and rights;
- involvement in genuine participation;
- access to support and services in relation to drug misuse, disability, unemployment, homelessness, mental illness etc.;
- treatment as individuals with individual needs and aspirations; and
- help to tackle discrimination and inequality.

Development of the Strategy by the council has been allocated distinct 'paths':

- the *Policy Development Path*, ensuring the council takes account of national youth initiatives and that its departments meet the needs of young people and work with others who address those needs; and
- the *Community Development Path*, allowing for the gradual and increasing involvement of young people in the Youth Strategy.

Implementation will be achieved through a Youth Strategy Action Plan, which will also oversee development of the recommendations of the three task groups on employment and training; crime; and participation and consultation.

The Real Deal

The Real Deal project combined research and group-based work, consulting more than 150 young people over eight months about their views on politics, social exclusion and the Government policies that affect them. The groups were recruited through Centrepoint and Save the Children Fund projects.

Five core themes were agreed at the start of the project:

- leisure and social activities;
- community and a sense of belonging;
- education;
- employment and training; and
- transitions to adulthood.

A sixth topic – government and decision making – emerged as an issue as the project progressed.

Impact
One of the objectives of the Real Deal project was to contribute to the development of communication and presentational skills amongst the young people involved. Sustaining group work over time was vital to achieving this aim. The extent to which this was achieved was dependent upon the skill of those working with the young people and the degree to which young people felt able to participate in presentations and public events.

A large proportion of the young people felt that they gained significantly from being involved in the Real Deal.

Youth Consultation, Birmingham City Council

The consultation process followed a joint report from the Chief Executive and the Director of Leisure and Community Services, outlining what they saw as the first steps in a strategy to improve the authority's dialogue with young people and the response from its services to meet their needs.

A city-wide series of consultation meetings was held with young people, on an area or neighbourhood basis. These were open to all local young residents. Some of the meetings were specifically targeted and structured to meet the needs of particular groups of young people, for example young Asian women. A total of over 500 young people aged between 13 and 21 were eventually involved in the process.

The ideas, issues, complaints and areas of concern were broken down into three main areas:

- local issues relevant to the area in which they lived;
- city-wide issues relating to council services or other more general concerns; and
- issues concerning young people's general status and situation within their neighbourhood, city or society as a whole.

Impact
Although some of the young people found the experience of sustained group discussion and expressing their views quite alien and difficult, in every group there were those who wanted to continue the process of engaging in planning and decision making. Many were highly motivated and had clear ideas about the contribution that they could make.

It was obvious that many young people feel disenfranchised and marginalised by current decision making, and have a wish to become involved if the structure by which they are able to do so is relevant to their needs. There was a widespread fear that nothing further would happen beyond these meetings, and that a lack of resources would prohibit progress.

Models of participation are now being devised, with a view to involving young people in deciding how best to develop the idea.

Action is being taken where appropriate on the local and city-wide issues raised during discussion.

Annex J: Detailed proposals on benefits for young people at risk

An expert meeting convened by the PAT identified a number of areas where changes to the delivery of benefits for young people at risk might assist in creating a more cohesive and responsive service.

Detailed proposals included:

- reviewing the present system used to establish whether a young person is estranged from their parents or person acting in the place of their parents. One suggestion is to accept a young person's word that they are estranged but only allow a claim to benefit to continue beyond four weeks if a specialist advice agency concluded after discussion with the young person that they were genuinely estranged;

- looking at how advice and guidance on benefit entitlement conditions can be incorporated in the support provided to young people who are experiencing emotional problems, to help to create a secure basis for a return to learning or work; and

- looking at ways to improve the Benefits Agency and Employment Service performance in dealing with young people in crisis. This could include revising guidance and reviewing training for specialist and other staff. It was also suggested that this could include consideration of training to an external accreditation standard for those dealing with vulnerable young people.

Notes

1 P. Gregg, K. Hansen and J. Wadsworth *The rise of the workless household,* in: P. Gregg and J. Wadsworth (editors), *The State of Working Britain,* Manchester University Press, 1999.

2 *Education and Labour Market Status of Young People in England aged 16–18, 1992 to 1998,* DfEE Statistical Bulletin, 11/99, October 1999. This signifies a six per cent increase in the previous year's figures, quoted in the SEU's *Bridging the Gap* report.

3 DfEE *Statistical First Release no. 35,* 1999.

4 OECD *Education at a Glance,* 1997.

5 ONS *Labour Force Survey 1997/98,* TSO, 1998.

6 SEU, *Teenage Pregnancy* (Cm 4342), TSO, 1999b.

7 Safe on the Streets Research Team *Still Running: children on the streets in the UK,* The Children's Society, 1999.

8 *Annual report on the state of the drugs problem in the European Union,* EMCDDA, 1998.

9 J. Graham and B. Bowling *Young people and Crime,* Home Office Research Study No.145, TSO, 1995.

10 P. Mayhew, P. and J.J. van Dijk *Criminal Victimisation in Eleven Industrialised Countries: Key findings from the 1996 International Crime Victim Survey,* 1997. (Countries included: Netherlands, England and Wales, USA, Canada, France, Scotland, Sweden, Switzerland, Finland, Austria and Northern Ireland.)

11 G. Bramley with S. Lancaster, D. Lomax, S. McIntosh and J. Russell, M. Evans and J. Atkins with M. Chell and J. Flatley *Where does public spending go? Pilot study to analyse the flows of public expenditure into local areas,* DETR, 1998.

12 See, for example, *Communities that Care (UK): a new kind of prevention programme,* 1997.

13 SEU *Bringing Britain together: a national strategy for neighbourhood renewal* (Cm 4045), TSO, 1998a.

14 J. Littlewood and B. Botting *Which children are 'at risk' and where are they?,* in: *Comprehensive Spending Review: Cross-Departmental Review of Provision for Young Children – Supporting Papers,* 1998.

15 ONS *Social Trends 28,* TSO, 1998.

16 P. Robinson *Education, training and the youth labour market,* in: P. Gregg and J. Wadsworth (editors) *The State of Working Britain,* Manchester University Press, 1999.

17 Ibid.

18 P. Gregg and J. Wadsworth *Job Tenure 1975–1998,* in: P. Gregg and J. Wadsworth (editors) op. cit., 1999.

19 T. Bentley and R. Gurumurthy *Destination Unknown: Engaging with the problems of marginalised youth,* Demos, 1999.

20 See, for example, J. Coleman *Key Data on Adolescence,* Trust for the Study of Adolescence, 1999.

21 J. Haskey *Children in Families Broken by Divorce,* Population Trends 61, OPCS/HMSO, 1991.

22 See, for example, L. Platt and M. Noble *Race, Place and Poverty: ethnic groups and low income distributions,* YPS/Joseph Rowntree Foundation, 1999.

23 K. Kiernan *The Legacy of Parental Divorce: social, economic and demographic experiences of adulthood,* Case Paper 1, London School of Economics, 1997. Divorce used to mean all parental separations.

24 J. Graham, comment on J. Bynner contribution to *Comprehensive Spending Review of Provision for Young Children – supporting papers,* volume 2, HMT, 1998.

25 F. McGlone, A. Park and K. Smith *Families in Kinship,* Family Policy Studies Centre, 1998.

26 DSS *Opportunity for all: tackling poverty and social exclusion,* First Annual Report 1999 (Cm 4445), TSO, 1999.

27 ONS *Labour Force Survey 1998/99,* TSO, 1999.

28 *Statistical First Release No. 35,* DfEE, 1999.

29 *Statistics of Education, Special Educational Needs in England, Statistical Bulletin 12/99,* DfEE, 1999.

30 *Education and Labour Market Status of Young People in England aged 16–18, 1992 to 1998,* DfEE Statistical Bulletin, 11/99, October 1999.

31 Safe on the Streets Research Team *Still Running: children on the streets in the UK,* The Children's Society, 1999.

32 Eurostat.

33 HO *British Crime Survey,* 1996.

34 E. Goddard and V. Higgins *Smoking, drinking and drug use among young people in 1998,* ONS, 1999.

35 M. Ramsay and S. Partridge *Drug Misuse Declared in 1998: Results from the British Crime Survey,* Home Office Research Study No. 197, 1999.

36 HO *British Crime Survey,* TSO, 1998.

37 J. Graham and B. Bowling *Young people and crime,* Home Office Research Study No.145, TSO, 1995.

38 *Young prisoners: a thematic review of HM Chief Inspector of Prisons for England and Wales,* HO, 1997.

39 *Education at a Glance,* OECD, 1997.

40 *Education across the EU,* Eurostat, 1998. Note: International comparisons of attainment are complicated by countries having different systems of assessment. The data here uses the International Standard classification of Education, but the results should still be treated with caution.

41 P. Gregg, K. Hansen and J. Wadsworth *The rise of the workless household,* in: P. Gregg and J. Wadsworth (editors), *The State of Working Britain,* Manchester University Press, 1999.

42 SEU *Bridging the Gap: new opportunities for 16–18 year olds not in education, employment or training* (Cm 4405), TSO, 1999a.

43 *Annual report on the state of the drugs problem in the European Union,* EMCDDA, 1998.

44 P. Mayhew, P. and J.J. van Dijk *Criminal Victimisation in Eleven Industrialised Countries: Key findings from the 1996 International Crime Victim Survey,* 1997. Countries included Netherlands, England and Wales, USA, Canada, France, Scotland, Sweden, Switzerland, Finland, Austria and Northern Ireland.

45 Poor households are defined as those with a total income below half the national average after housing costs. DSS *Opportunity for all: tackling poverty and social exclusion,* First Annual Report 1999 (Cm 4445), TSO, 1999.

46 *Welfare Reform Focus File No. 7,* DSS, 1997.

47 *Statistics of Education, Special Educational Needs in England, Statistical Bulletin 12/99,* DfEE, 1999. In part this may reflect increased awareness of the problem and the benefits of having a statement. Rising proportion of children with SEN, whether with or without a statement, may reflect changes other than in objective levels of educational need, such as changes in educational policy and practice or changes in thresholds and definitions of what constitutes need.

48 SEU *Truancy and School Exclusion* (Cm 3957), TSO, 1998b.

49 Standing Conference on Drug Abuse (SCODA) and Children's Legal Centre, *Young People and Drugs,* 1999.

50 C. Mirrlees-Black, T. Budd, S. Partridge and P. Mayhew *The 1998 British Crime Survey,* Home Office Statistical Bulletin 21/98, GSS, 1999.

51 J. Graham and B. Bowling *Young People and Crime,* Home Office Research Study No. 145, HMSO, 1995.

52 This table has been adapted from Communities that Care (UK), but expanded to incorporate two additional youth problems – mental health problems and homelessness. The simplified list of risk factors has also been reduced to those which we considered to be key.

53 The most important risk factors connected with offending are delinquent peers, poor parental supervision, truancy, delinquent siblings (for males), exclusion from school and (for females) weak attachment to family and school. J. Graham and B. Bowling *Young People and Crime,* Home Office Research Study No. 145, HMSO, 1995.

54 Source: K. Kiernan *Transition to Parenthood: young mothers, young fathers: associated factors and later life experiences,* London School of Economics, 1995.

55 Consisting of young people of black African-Caribbean, Asian and mixed racial origin. *Patterns and Outcomes in Child Placement,* DH, 1991.

56 D. Gillborn *Exclusion from school,* 1996.

57 ONS *Labour Force Survey 1997/98,* TSO, 1998.

58 B. Chatrik *New Deal – Fair Deal? Black young people in the Labour Market,* Barnardo's/Children's Society/Youth Aid, 1997.

59 Ibid.

60 *Centrepoint statistics April 1998 – March 1999,* Centrepoint, 1999.

61 *Statewatch,* 1998.

62 See, for example, *Communities that Care (UK): a new kind of prevention programme,* 1997.

63 J. Graham and B. Bowling op. cit., 1995. It should be noted that these appear to be stronger factors in the desistance of young women from reoffending than young men.

64 The case study of Wayne is taken from: Safe on the Streets Research Team *Still Running: children on the streets in the UK,* The Children's Society, 1999.

65 SEU op. cit., 1999b.

66 DSS *Opportunity for all: tackling poverty and social exclusion,* First Annual Report 1999 (Cm 4445), TSO, 1999.

67 SEU op. cit., 1998b.

68 SEU op. cit., 1999a.

69 SEU op. cit., 1999b.

70 *Parents in poor neighbourhoods*, BMRB, 1999.

71 *The Real Deal: what young people really think about government, politics and social exclusion*, Demos, 1999.

72 DfEE *Jobs for All: report of the PAT on Jobs*, 1999.

73 HO *Supporting Families*, TSO, 1998; and HO *Supporting Families: summary of responses to the consultation document*, TSO, 1999.

74 D. Ghate and A. Hagell *Parenting in poor environments: stress, coping and support*, Policy Research Bureau, forthcoming.

75 Ibid.

76 DfEE *Sure Start: making a difference for children and families*, TSO, 1999.

77 See: HO op. cit., 1998; and HO op. cit., 1999.

78 *The Real Deal: what young people really think about government, politics and social exclusion*, Demos, 1999.

79 D. Roker and J. Coleman *Teenagers in the Family*, Trust for the Study of Adolescence, 1998.

80 T. Bentley and R. Gurumurthy *Destination Unknown: Engaging with the problems of marginalised youth*, Demos, 1999.

81 Safe on the Streets Research Team *Still Running: children on the streets in the UK*, The Children's Society, 1999.

82 See, for example, *Moving on up: how youth work raises achievement and promotes social inclusion*, DfEE/National Youth Agency, 1998.

83 DfEE *Learning to Succeed: a new framework for post-16 learning* (Cm 4392), TSO, 1999; SEU op. cit., 1999b; *Connexions: the best start in life for every young person*, DfEE, 2000.

84 *Children in Mind*, Audit Commission, 1999.

85 N. Madge *Abuse and Survival: a fact file*, Prince's Trust, 1997.

86 Although the NHS does purchase places in beds for patients in the private sector.

87 *Bright Futures: promoting children and young people's mental health*, Mental Health Foundation, 1999.

88 SEU op. cit., 1999b.

89 UK Anti-Drugs Co-ordination Unit *Tackling Drugs to Build a Better Britain* (Cm 3945), TSO, 1998.

90 DH, *Saving Lives: Our Healthier Nation* (Cm 4386), TSO, 1999.

91 P. Wiles, S. Holdaway, P. Marsh, R. Hammersley, J. Dignan, N. Davidson and J. Hine *Interim Evaluation of YOTs*, Sheffield University and Hull University, 1999.

92 C. Mirrlees-Black, T. Budd, S. Partridge and P. Mayhew *The 1998 British Crime Survey*, Home Office Statistical Bulletin 21/98, GSS, 1999.

93 *The Stephen Lawrence Inquiry: report of an inquiry by Sir William Macpherson* (Cm 4262-I), TSO, 1999.

94 *Sort It Out! Reforming the benefit system for 16 and 17 year olds*, COYPSS, 1999.

95 The DETR revised *Code of Guidance for Local Authorities on the Allocation of Accommodation and Homelessness* – currently in draft – recommends that local authorities consider both care leavers and 16 and 17 year olds with no backup support as vulnerable under the homelessness legislation.

96 V. White and D. Levison *Housing Benefit and the Private Rented Sector*, DETR, 1999. This research looked at six local authority areas.

97 *People Like Us: the report of the review of the safeguards of children living away from home*, TSO, 1997.

98 DH *Me, Survive, Out there?*, TSO, 1999.

99 *The Real Deal: what young people really think about government, politics and social exclusion*, Demos, 1999.

100 Ibid.

101 G. Bramley with S. Lancaster, D. Lomax, S. McIntosh and J. Russell, M. Evans and J. Atkins with M. Chell and J. Flatley *Where does public spending go? Pilot study to analyse the flows of public expenditure into local areas*, DETR, 1998.

102 The researchers included in this category spending on child benefit, 50 per cent of income support for those other than the unemployed, 50 per cent of family credit, 40 per cent of council tax benefit, 40 per cent of housing benefit, all spending on primary and special schools, 60 per cent of spending on secondary schools and other spending by local education authorities.

103 The researchers included in this category 40 per cent of spending on secondary schools and all spending on further and higher education and on TECs and probation.

104 One exception to this is on spending on social services, where the resource allocation formula is informed by the York deprivation index.

105 DH *Modernising Social Services: promoting independence, improving performance, raising standards* (Cm 4169), TSO, 1998.

106 *Measuring Success: Young Citizens Programme: interim operational report, November 1997 – October 1998*, Hertfordshire County Council, 1998.

107 Adapted from: *Comparative study of youth policies and legislation in states party to the European Cultural Convention of the Council of Europe,* Council of Europe, Youth Directorate, 1998.

108 This denotes that one Minister – not necessarily named as a 'Minister for Youth' – has overall responsibility for co-ordinating policy on youth issues.

109 This denotes that one department – not necessarily named as a 'Department for Youth' – has overall responsibility for co-ordinating policy on youth issues.

110 Or equivalent.

111 Denoting a clearly stated overarching Government youth policy.

112 Flemish-speaking community.

113 No information available.

114 Proposals in train for a national youth policy at time of report.

115 SEU op. cit., 1999a.

116 SEU op. cit., 1999b.

117 P. Gregg *The Impact of Unemployment and Job Loss on Future Earnings* in: *Persistent Poverty and Lifetime Inequality: the Evidence,* CASE/HMT, 1999.

118 SEU op. cit., 1998b.

119 DH op. cit., 1999.

120 In this section, references to 'young people' can be taken to include children and young people under the age of 18.

121 SEU op. cit., 1999a.

122 DfEE *Connexions: the best start in life for every young person,* DfEE, 2000.

123 DfEE, report of PAT 11, *Building Learning Communities: improving the educational chances of children and young people from disadvantaged areas,* 2000.

124 See, for example, J. Smith and I. Bruegel *Taking Risks: an analysis of the risks of homelessness for young people in London,* report to the Safe in the City Partnership, 1999.

125 SEU op. cit., 1999a.

126 SEU op. cit., 1999b.

127 *Delivering Benefits to Unemployed 16 and 17 year olds,* Research Report, DSS, 1997; and *The Effects of Jobseeker's Allowance on 16 and 17 Year Olds,* DfEE 1998.

128 M. Liddle *Wasted Lives: counting the cost of juvenile offending,* NACRO/The Prince's Trust, 1998.

129 Policy Directions are made to the five Lottery distributors: Sport England; the Arts Council of England; the National Heritage Memorial Fund; the National Lotteries Charities Board; and the New Opportunities Fund. Directions are made under Section 26(1) of the National Lottery etc. Act, 1993 (as amended).

130 *Connexions: the best start in life for every young person,* DfEE, 2000.

131 *Report of the Policy Action Team on Community Self-help,* HO, Active Community Unit, 1999.

132 *Arts and Sport: Policy Action Team 10: a report to the Social Exclusion Unit,* DCMS, 1999.

133 *Listen Up, A dialogue with young men and young women* will be published shortly by the HO and the Women's Unit.

134 Much of the analysis in this paper draws on material produced by: the Institute for Public Policy Research; the National Youth Agency; the Commission for Racial Equality; the UK Anti-Drugs Co-ordination Unit; P. Loftman and M. Beazley *Race and Regeneration,* LGIU, 1998; and a paper by the London Development Partnership on Black and Ethnic minorities.

135 P. Loftman and M. Beazley, *Race and Regeneration,* LGIU, 1998.

136 J. Lakey *Neighbourhoods and Housing,* in: T. Modood, R. Berthoud, J. Lakey, J. Nazroo, P. Smith, S. Virdee and S. Beishon *Ethnic Minorities in Britain: diversity and disadvantage,* PSI, 1997.

137 SEU op. cit., 1998a.

138 ONS *Social Trends 28,* TSO, 1998.

139 Ibid.

140 R. Berthoud and S. Beishon *People, Families and Households,* in: T. Modood, et al, op. cit., 1997.

141 Ibid.

142 *Patterns and Outcomes in Child Placement,* DH, 1991.

143 Based on R. Berthoud *Income and Standards of Living,* in: T. Modood, et al, op. cit., 1997.

144 T. Modood, et al, op. cit., 1997.

145 ONS *Mortality Statistics: perinatal and infant: social and biological factors*, Series DH3, TSO, 1997.

146 SEU op. cit., 1999b.

147 SEU op. cit., 1999b.

148 *Centrepoint statistics* April 1998 – March 1999, Centrepoint, 1999.

149 J. Lakey *Neighbourhoods and Housing*, in: T. Modood, et al, op. cit., 1997.

150 Ibid.

151 Ibid.

152 Ibid.

153 Ibid.

154 SEU op. cit., 1999a. From available information, girls appear generally to outperform boys across all ethnic groups – see OFSTED, *Raising the Attainment of Ethnic Minority Pupils*, HMI 170, 1999.

155 D. Gillborn and C. Gipps *Recent Research on the Achievements of Ethnic Minority Pupils*, OFSTED, 1996.

156 Ibid.

157 Ibid.

158 D. Gillborn *Exclusion from school*, 1996.

159 Commission for Racial Equality *Young People in Britain*, CRE Factsheet, 1998.

160 SEU op. cit., 1999a.

161 T. Modood *Unemployment*, in: T. Modood, R. Berthoud, J. Lakey, J. Nazroo, P. Smith, S. Virdee and S. Beishon *Ethnic Minorities in Britain: diversity and disadvantage*, PSI, 1997.

162 *Youth Cohort Study*, cohort 9, sweep 1.

163 ONS *Labour Force Survey, 1997*, TSO, 1998 and *Family and Working Lives Survey, 1994/95*, TSO, 1996.

164 ONS *Labour Force Survey 1997/98*, TSO, 1998.

165 A. Percy *Ethnicity and Victimisation: findings from the 1996 British Crime Survey*, Home Office Statistical Bulletin Issue 6/98, 1998.

166 *Statistics on Race and the Criminal Justice System*, HO, 1999.

167 HO *Prison Statistics, England and Wales, 1998*, TSO, 1999.

168 M. Ramsay and J. Spiller *Drug Misuse Declared in 1996: Latest results from the British Crime Survey*, Home Office Research Study No. 172, 1997.

169 This and all other such attributed quotes come from: *Parents in poor neighbourhoods*, BMRB, 1999.

170 ONS *Social Trends 30, 2000 Edition*, TSO, 2000.

171 *Welfare Reform Focus File No.7*, DSS, 1997.

172 J. Haskey *Children in Families Broken by Divorce*, Population Trends 61, OPCS/HMSO, 1991.

173 ONS *Marriage, divorce and adoption statistics, England and Wales, 1995 Series FM2 no.23*, TSO, 1998.

174 *Welfare Reform Focus File No.7*, DSS, 1997.

175 F. McGlone *A Guide to Family Issues*, Family Briefing Paper 2, Family Policy Studies Centre, 1997.

176 Office of Population Censuses and Surveys (now ONS), *1992 General Household Survey*, HMSO, 1994.

177 C. Howarth, P. Kenway, G. Palmer and C. Street *Monitoring Poverty and Social Exclusion: Labour's inheritance*, New Policy Institute/Joseph Rowntree Foundation, 1999.

178 K. Kiernan *The Legacy of Parental Divorce: social, economic and demographic experiences of adulthood*, Case Paper 1, London School of Economics, 1997. Divorce used to mean all parental separations.

179 J. Graham, comment on J. Bynner contribution to *Comprehensive Spending Review of Provision for Young Children – supporting papers*, volume 2, HMT, 1998.

180 DSS *Households Below Average Income 1994/5–1997/8*, TSO, 1999.

181 Poor households are defined as those with a total income below half the national average after housing costs. DSS *Opportunity for all: tackling poverty and social exclusion*, First Annual Report 1999 (Cm 4445), TSO, 1999.

182 P. Gregg, K. Hansen and J. Wadsworth *The Rise of the Workless Household*, in: P. Gregg and J. Wadsworth (editors) *The State of Working Britain*, Manchester University Press, 1999.

183 *Households Below Average Income: a statistical analysis 1979–1996/7*, DSS, 1998.

184 P. Morgan *Farewell to the Family? Public policy and family breakdown in Britain and the USA*, 2nd edition, IEA Health and Welfare Unit, London, 1997.

185 SEU op. cit., 1999b.

186 V. Morrows and M. Richards *Transitions to adulthood: a family matter?*, Joseph Rowntree Foundation, 1996.

187 Safe on the Streets Research Team *Still Running: children on the streets in the UK*, The Children's Society, 1999.

188 DSS *Households Below Average Income 1994/5–1997/8*, TSO, 1999.

189 Based on data from the 1991 Census.

190 DSS *Households Below Average Income: a statistical analysis 1994/5 to 1997/8*, TSO, 1999.

191 C. Kagan, S. Lewis and P. Heaton *Caring to Work: accounts of working parents with disabled children*, Family Policy Studies Centre, 1998.

192 C. Oldman and B. Beresford *Home Unfit for Children: housing, disabled children and families*, The Policy Press, 1998.

193 D. Lawton *Complex Numbers: families with more than one disabled child*, Social Policy Report No. 8, University of York, 1998.

194 J. Warin, Y. Solomon, C. Lewis and W. Langford *Fathers, work and family life*, Family Policy Studies Centre with Joseph Rowntree Foundation, 1999.

195 SEU op. cit., 1999a.

196 SEU op. cit., 1999b.

197 J. Shropshire and S. Middleton *Small Expectations: Learning to be poor?*, Joseph Rowntree Foundation/YPS, 1999.

198 HO op. cit., 1998; and HO op. cit., 1999.

199 Policy Research Bureau: ongoing research.

200 Centre for the Study of the Child, the Family and the Law, University of Liverpool.

201 D. Roker and J. Coleman *Teenagers in the Family*, Trust for the Study of Adolescence, 1998.

202 J. Coleman *The Parenting of Adolescents in Britain Today* in: *Children in Society*, Volume 11, 1997.

203 *Comparative study of youth policies and legislation in states party to the European Cultural Convention of the Council of Europe*, Council of Europe, Youth Directorate, 1998.

204 This denotes that one Minister – not necessarily named as a 'Minister for Youth' – has overall responsibility for co-ordinating policy on youth issues.

205 This denotes that one department – not necessarily named as a 'Department for Youth' – has overall responsibility for co-ordinating policy on youth issues.

206 Or equivalent.

207 Denoting a clearly stated overarching Government youth policy.

208 Flemish-speaking community.

209 No information available.

210 Proposals in train for a national youth policy at time of report.

CABI/00 - 5342/0003/D14.4